EDWARD I
AND CRIMINAL LAW

THE WILES LECTURES
GIVEN AT THE QUEEN'S UNIVERSITY
BELFAST 1958

EDWARD I

AND

CRIMINAL LAW

BY

T. F. T. PLUCKNETT

*Professor of Legal History in the
University of London*

CAMBRIDGE
AT THE UNIVERSITY PRESS
1960

CAMBRIDGE UNIVERSITY PRESS
Cambridge, New York, Melbourne, Madrid, Cape Town, Singapore, São Paulo, Delhi

Cambridge University Press
The Edinburgh Building, Cambridge CB2 8RU, UK

Published in the United States of America by Cambridge University Press, New York

www.cambridge.org
Information on this title: www.cambridge.org/9780521059671

© Cambridge University Press 1960

First published 1960
This digitally printed version 2008

A catalogue record for this publication is available from the British Library

ISBN 978-0-521-05967-1 hardback
ISBN 978-0-521-08565-6 paperback

CONTENTS

PREFACE

The four lectures which make up this little book were delivered in May 1958 at the Queen's University of Belfast in the series of Wiles Lectures on the History of Civilisation.

To that imaginative as well as munificent foundation I am grateful, first for the honour of election to their lectureship, and secondly for their forethought in assembling so distinguished a gathering of lawyers and historians, not only from the Queen's University of Belfast, but also from Eire, England and France. The subsequent discussions among the company were of great interest, and have contributed to the final form in which the lectures now appear.

T. F. T. P.

CHAPTER I

REPARATION AND THE VICTIM

WHEN we think of Edward I we can hardly separate him from the age in which he lived. Nor is it altogether necessary that we should. He was a great king, and it was a great age, and for most purposes that is enough. The king and the age—the man and the environment— were inseparable then, and we need not try to put them asunder now. To some it may seem proper to place the figure of Edward I high among the heroes of Church and State portrayed in stained glass, which for succeeding centuries has shown our respect, and his worth; to others (especially to some modern historians) he seems 'a little lower than the angels'—a good deal lower, in fact—and becomes noticeably more immersed in an environment which may be painted in darker colours. We need not be unduly alarmed; Edward I never set himself up as a teacher of mankind, and, as far as we can know, he only claimed to represent the current thought of his age. If we therefore examine the age in which he lived we may hope to find a contemporary estimation of the problems which faced him, whether they be religious, social, civil or criminal, and watch the endeavours of a well-informed, but not an expert, ruler to deal with them.

The appropriate machinery lay close at hand—legislation. In France, in England, in Spain, and elsewhere, when a large problem had to be tackled in broad and general terms, it was a 'statute' or 'ordonnance' or some such device which embodied the king's commands to his lieutenants and to his people. There is no need to conceal the fact that 'statutes' and their like could bring with them some serious problems, some of which are not yet entirely solved. The political scientist will examine critically the idea of 'legislation'; the theologian will not be immediately satisfied that what it has created is truly 'law'; and the lawyer is not always certain what he should do with it—whatever one calls it—even in our own day: the problem of 'interpretation' is still with us. These were hazards which a legislator must nevertheless accept if he is to do anything, and it seems agreed in the Middle Ages that a ruler cannot avoid his duty to provide his people with justice.

Legislation is a powerful weapon; it is difficult to say that it is confined by any definite limits. Nevertheless, it is also an uncertain one, and it is by no means fore-seeable what its effects may be, especially when young unskilful hands are fumbling with a strange new toy. Moreover, a legislator stands at a particular moment, an unknown past behind him, an inscrutable future before him. We, who live at a safe distance and need not be overmuch worried by the problems which beset Edward I, can make use of our advantages. His past and his future are both open to us, although he was but dimly aware of the one, and utterly ignorant of the other. That knowledge is for us to use. We can see his problems more clearly than he did; whether we shall judge them more wisely is another matter. The way to tackle the problems which confronted Edward I at the end of the thirteenth century seems tolerably clear. First, there is the past which piled up mountains of difficulties, beneath which perhaps lay concealed some useful clues—if only they could be unearthed. Then we must consider the thought of those who up to now had succeeded in reaching some sort of conclusion—however tentative—about crime and criminal law. Next we must see what sort of results Edward I derived from his consideration of these matters, if indeed he or his advisers had given them adequate consideration. Finally, we must give thought to that ineluctable consequence of human action—its bearing on the future, and its results, good or bad, for the development of the criminal law.

When we look at our earliest Anglo-Saxon laws, they show us a world so different from ours that it is difficult to think of them as in any way relevant to our inquiry. Their most obvious characteristic, and their most significant one, is the all but total absence of any arrangement in them. No doubt there is a certain association of ideas, especially in the later Anglo-Saxon laws, which supplies some modicum of unity in them, at least for short intervals. Nor can we excuse this absence as merely the unskilful presentation of its laws by a nation which was still young in the legislative art. It is more than a question of form, and much more than a question of literary tricks and graces. We must regard it as showing that the draftsmen of these laws had not yet achieved the first rudiments of a vocabulary which would enable them to analyse the law into such categories as 'crime', 'tort', 'property', 'procedure' and the like, which are indis-

I-2

pensable if we are to consider, for however short a while, some point of law and its relationship with other legal rules and concepts. When we have to evaluate the work which has been preserved in the Anglo-Saxon laws, it should be remembered that its framers and draftsmen had to work without those tools of legal analysis and nomenclature which seem to us quite essential if our thoughts are to be directed accurately and usefully to the law and its problems.

That last point should also be considered from another point of view, that of Roman law. There we have a problem which will constantly meet us as we consider the course of English legal history. When we first have texts which purport to come from the kingdom of Kent and from the reign of its king Æthelberht, Roman law already had a thousand years of history behind it. A vast treasure of tried and tested legal results lay to hand in the *Corpus Juris* of Justinian, the fruit of the age-long experience of the City. As the age grew darker, it seemed almost miraculous that such a treasury of law should have been assembled and should be within the reach of at least some rare and favoured spirits, even if it be only in the much diluted form of the *Breviarium Alaricianum*.[1] Our own Aldhelm found that work heavy going, but it served to keep him away from a Christmas

---

[1] It has been supposed that Aldhelm took this book from Canterbury (where he read it) to Malmesbury (of which house he later became abbot), and that William of Malmesbury (who died in 1143) made a copy much later which is now in the Bodleian (Selden B. 16); from which copy it would seem that Aldhelm had been reading the *Breviarium Alaricianum* (M. R. James, *Two Ancient English Scholars*, pp. 13–14; F. M. Stenton, *Anglo-Saxon England*, p. 181; Pollock and Maitland, *History of English Law*, vol. I, p. xxxii, n. 2).

party, nevertheless. The ready-made results of Roman law were often an immediate attraction to those scholars who made acquaintance with them for the first time. But much more profound in its ultimate result was the matchless gift of method.

We may distinguish, although we cannot altogether separate, these two aspects of Roman law. A medieval jurist or statesman may very well have been tempted to borrow the language or even the institutions of a foreign system whose results were there to be had for the taking, much as a modern schoolboy may be tempted to look up the answers at the end of the book. In either case the result is apt to be the same: the borrower, the taker of the short cut, will generally reveal himself when we examine carefully the nature of his new-won spoil. Did he invent it himself? Is it the result of his own thought and the outcome of his own experience? Or is it the work of other men (one might almost say, the product of a different culture) which the borrower has understood but imperfectly, if at all? The spread throughout the world of Roman law, like the much later spread of English parliamentary institutions, has not always been the rational outcome of the borrowers' own legal or political history.

In a famous passage Maitland has reminded us of how Glanvill came to distinguish civil from criminal causes,[1] and how in the next century Bracton learnt much from the canonist Bernard of Pavia.[2] It had to be

---

[1] Pollock and Maitland, *History of English Law*, vol. II, p. 477.

[2] *Ibid.* It is now suggested that Bracton in fact used Raymond of Penafort, who had been much indebted to Bernard of Pavia: see F. Schulz, 'Bracton and Raymond de Penafort', *Law Quarterly Review*, vol. LXI (1945), p. 286.

admitted that before the conquest 'what we may call the criminal law of England...was also the law of "torts" or civil wrongs',[1] and that, in spite of the prowess of Glanvill and Bracton, 'even at the present day we can hardly say that *crime* is one of the technical terms of our law'.[2]

The deeper and more lasting influence of Roman law was exerted in a more subtle and permanent manner, not in the transplanting of this or that turn of language, or of some useful legal device, but in the whole attitude with which it approached the problems of law. The spirit of a body of law, which was often alien in time and place to those who came into contact with it, was not to be learned in a day. The professional scholars acquired it first, and from the civilians and canonists (who necessarily spent much time in study of the books of Justinian) the new spirit spread to the theologians. In practice, the problem was how to write a book; but in its broadest aspect, the systematisation and orderly presentation of human knowledge was involved. To present theological, or legal, doctrine as a logical whole is in itself a searching test; its orderly arrangement can only be attempted after long and detailed study which is itself a criticism as well as an exposition.

The laws of the Anglo-Saxon kings have been scrutinised with great care by those scholars who are con-

---

[1] Pollock and Maitland, vol. II, p. 449.

[2] *Ibid.* vol. II, p. 573. On this there are some pertinent remarks in the chapter on 'Tort and Crime' in the late Sir Percy Winfield's *Province of the Law of Tort* (1931); on indictable trespasses see my 'Commentary on the Indictments' in B. H. Putnam, *Proceedings before the Justices of the Peace* (Ames Foundation), pp. cxxxiii ff. at clvi.

cerned to find the faintest traces of Roman influence, and the result of their search has been to show how little Roman influence is discernible. 'Eyes, carefully trained, have minutely scrutinized the Anglo-Saxon legal texts without finding the least trace of a Roman rule outside the ecclesiastical sphere.'[1] So wrote Maitland, and it is a reasonably accurate judgement.[2] It is certainly clear beyond doubt that there is no sign in the Anglo-Saxon laws that the greatest and most general lesson of Roman law had been learned: the texts present no trace whatever of any attempt to arrange their material. The nearest we get to a systematic treatment of a subject is towards the end of the period, when a number of provisions upon the same matter are put together in a roughly narrative form. The great lack which is so conspicuous is any systematic analysis of legal ideas.

If we look at our oldest surviving laws, those of King Æthelberht, it becomes clear how the draftsman went about the novel task of putting together the first piece of legislation in England. The general heading refers to the matters that follow as 'the dooms which King Æthelberht set up in Augustine's day'. There follow ninety clauses, mostly very short, whose arrangement discloses some slight association of ideas as a basis for their arrangement, but nothing more. The first clause contains a *calculus* of some sort which has to be guessed from the

---

[1] F. W. Maitland, *Historical Essays* (ed. H. M. Cam), p. 100.
[2] Some mercantile passages about shipping seem Roman (Pollock and Maitland, vol. I, pp. 102–3 n.) and Maitland himself regards the idea of treason as romanesque: *ibid.* vol. II, p. 503; T. F. T. Plucknett, 'Roman Law and English Common Law', *University of Toronto Law Journal*, vol. III, p. 26.

allusive terms which are used: 'God's property and the Church's, twelvefold; a bishop's, elevenfold; a priest's, ninefold; a deacon's, sixfold; a clerk's, threefold; Church-frith, twofold; maethl-frith, twofold.'[1] The payments (which are described as multiples of a 'basic charge', so to speak) seem to depend upon the value of the goods stolen, which the offender ought to restore 'twelvefold', or in whatever other proportion is indicated in the text just quoted. Although the text does not say why these sums should be paid, this conjecture[2] seems to be justified by the facts that the table quoted does not contain the term *wer*, nor the term *bot*, but simply the word *gylde*. The table seems therefore to be not concerned with those slayings which were the primary source of calculations based upon the *wer*, nor with those physical injuries which offenders atoned for by offering *bot* or compensation; there remains the plausible conjecture that it deals with property stolen from the various grades of churchmen mentioned—and we must remember that the kingdom of Kent had just embraced a new religion, and therefore had to provide for its ministers in its laws. The insertion of a new category of men into its social and legal system could be effected by only one means—legislation.

That may very well have been the principal consideration which drove Æthelberht to the desperate device of committing himself to legislation; but having engaged in

[1] Text in F. Liebermann, *Gesetze der Angelsachsen*, vol. I, p. 3, where the citation of this passage is 'Abt. I'; cf. *ibid.* vol. III, p. 4. The word *maethl* is a sixteenth-century conjecture.

[2] Bede himself, *Ecclesiastical History* (ed. C. Plummer, vol. II, p. 5), adopted this view.

that perilous enterprise, the opportunity was also a
temptation to legislate on other matters at the same
time. These other matters are highly miscellaneous; but
many of them would now be classed as criminal. Some
traces of arrangement are discernible. Thus, cc. 2–12
seem all to deal with sums of money due to the king.
From c. 4 which is among them it will be noticed that
robbing the king is somewhat less costly than robbing
the Church or a bishop (c. 1), and from other chapters
that payments become due to the king for robbery and
violence to his servants. In contrast with these eleven
chapters dealing with the king, the next two are enough
to deal with the rights of an *eorl* or nobleman (cc. 13
and 14); the simple freeman (*ceorl*), on the other hand,
seems to occupy an inordinate amount of space (cc. 15–
85). There were many exciting things that might happen
to him: and the phrase 'simple freeman' hardly expresses adequately the complexity and variety of social
structure within which the *ceorl* lived and worked. Thus
the lord would be entitled to eighty, sixty, or forty shillings according as to whether it was his first-, second- or
third-class *laet*[1] who was slain (c. 26); and dealings might
indeed involve the *mund* (protection) of a first-, second-,
third- or fourth-class widow (c. 75). It is in the extended
treatment of the simple freeman that we find some of the
most remarkable provisions in Æthelberht's laws which
seem to show that its basis had not yet had time to
become Christian. There are passages which seem to

---

[1] On the meaning of this *hapax legomenon* in the Anglo-Saxon laws see
Liebermann, *Gesetze*, vol. II, p. 564, and F. L. Attenborough, *Laws of the
Earliest English Kings*, p. 177; the assumption seems to be that the lord of
the *laet* received the payment.

indicate that marriage by capture was still possible (c. 82),[1] and that where the modern divorce court might award damages, Æthelberht would regard it a more suitable remedy for the seducer to pay the wife's[2] *wergild* and supply the injured husband with a new wife bought, paid for, and delivered at the seducer's expense (c. 31). No one would regard all this as easily compatible with the views of Christian marriage which were, in the fulness of time, to become the classical common law.

There are still other passages which bear unmistakable marks of antiquity. It seems sometimes to be asserted that liability may attach to a weapon which had become involved in unlawful enterprises, and that the lender of such weapons may have to meet a considerable liability if those weapons were used to slay a man, or in furtherance of a highway robbery (cc. 20, 19). That is not merely the thought of the year 600 or thereabouts: the same notions are to be found in the much more sophisticated laws of King Alfred shortly before the year 900. Indeed, shortly before the Conquest, Canute himself ventured to adopt a more modern attitude to those who do mischief with another man's weapon which came casually into their hands, and enacted[3] that the man who did the harm must pay for it; but the owner of the weapon must clear himself of any complicity in the affair.[4]

[1] Cf. Pollock and Maitland, vol. II, p. 365, n. 5.

[2] Attenborough, Liebermann and Schmidt differ upon the interpretation of this passage.   [3] II Canute 75. Cf. Alfred 19 § 2.

[4] The idea that there was some sort of presumption, which the lender ought to rebut, makes an early appearance in Alfred 19 § 2. Earlier still, the loan of a weapon which caused damage involved the lender in the payment of *bot*, without any complicity being alleged: Æthelberht 19, 20.

The wording of the paragraph seems to be arguing with the reader, who may not be immediately convinced of the policy of the law; one is left with the feeling that possibly the rule set up proceeds not only from an ancient tradition, but also from the law's suspicion, in its worldly wisdom, that if a crime is committed with a man's weapon, he can reasonably be put to prove that he is blameless in the matter.

The most striking passages of the laws of Æthelberht, however, are those which consist of pre-ordained tariffs of payments which are deemed to be 'compensation' (*bot*) for various sorts of wrongs. Examples have already been given of those wrongs which entitle the king, or some other lord, to receive a payment for a wrong done to a servant or dependent which was also an affront to the king or lord with jurisdiction over him. A great many of the provisions here, however, set out the compensation payable to a man himself, apart from that due to his lord or master, in respect of personal injuries. The list begins at c. 33 and continues until c. 72 with an astonishing catalogue of the various ways of causing grievous bodily harm. Beginning with the hair of the head, we proceed through all sorts of injuries to the skull, ears, eyes, teeth, where the appropriate sum of money is attached to every injury—'for each of the four front teeth, six shillings; for each of the teeth which stand next to them, four shillings; then for each tooth which stands next to them, three shillings; and beyond that, one shilling for each tooth'. So too the text details the fingers, finger-nails and toes— and by this time (c. 71) it was possible to hazard a general rule instead of a tedious enumeration: 'for each of the other toes,' we are told, 'half of that laid down for the corresponding fingers shall be paid'. Here at least is a primitive rule designed to introduce a little bit of generality into what otherwise would be merely a disorderly enumeration—a tariff. A century later we find a sort of interpretation paragraph in the laws of Ine (who was king of Wessex *c.* 688–*c.* 726) when he explains that he uses the word 'thieves' when there are not more than seven, that he describes as 'marauders' (*hloð*) a band of seven to thirty-five, and as a 'raid' (*here*) an operation by a greater number of aggressors.[1] This useful remark seems to have provoked some textual difficulty,[2] but unhappily did not set the fashion for inserting interpretation clauses in later laws.

The general device of a tariff of payment, very roughly classified, thus occurs in our oldest body of laws, coming from the year 600 or very near it. Primitive as it seems, we still find much the same sort of thing in the laws of King Alfred, who died nearly three centuries later. Chapters 44–77 are in fact a long tariff of physical injuries which strikingly recalls the laws of Æthelberht. It is impossible to escape the problem which this presents to us. Was this legislation in the nature of an antiquarian revival? Do those chapters faithfully portray the best that Alfred and his age could contribute to the problem of crime and law? Would we be safe in concluding that the three centuries between the deaths of Æthelberht

---

[1] The gloss to the *Institutes*, dealing (much later) with words of multitude, was to explain that ten sheep, or four or five pigs, constitute a flock—to which a later hand added that three men may be a college: *Inst.* 2. 20. 18 *gl. si grex.*

[2] As to which see Liebermann, *Gesetze*, vol. I, p. 94, note **; Ine 13 §1.

and of Alfred had witnessed no change? (And here it is wise to avoid the word 'progress' with its philosophical implications.)

These are grave questions, but we can reasonably give Alfred the credit for at least understanding them. A modern historian has written a most impressive summary of Alfred and his place in history:

On any estimate [wrote Sir Frank Stenton] he was the most effective ruler who had appeared in western Europe since the death of Charlemagne. But beneath his preoccupation with duties, often of desperate urgency, there was always a sense of imponderable values. No other king of the Dark Ages ever set himself, like Alfred, to explore whatever in Christian antiquity might explain the problems of fate and free will, the divine purpose in ordering the world, and the ways by which man comes to knowledge.

His unique importance in the history of English letters comes from his conviction that a life without knowledge or reflection was unworthy of respect, and his determination to bring the thought of the past within the range of his subjects' understanding.[1]

As Sir Frank Stenton has remarked, there is a real link between Alfred's literary work and his laws.[2] The long and carefully composed prologue[3] which Alfred prefixed to them was put there in order to justify and clarify his approach to legislation, and to explain to us the spirit in which he worked. He begins with the Ten Commandments from Exodus xx, and continues (with the omission of purely narrative passages only) as far as Exodus xxiii. 13; then he turns to the New Testament,

[1] F. M. Stenton, *Anglo-Saxon England*, pp. 266–7.   [2] *Ibid.* pp. 272–3.
[3] Text in Liebermann, *Gesetze*, vol. I, pp. 26–46 (summary only in F. L. Attenborough, *Laws of the Earliest English Kings*, pp. 34–5).

and after a short passage from Matthew v. 17 he takes up Acts xv. 23–9, and concludes with the golden rule from Matthew vii. 12. It is obvious from his introduction and the extracts in it that Alfred was looking for clear statements upon important legal matters, and in the last words of his introduction (which serve to present his own legislation) it is expressly stated that Alfred is conscious of his place in the stream of history, of the good enactments of his predecessors which he has collected, although there are others which he has rejected, and of the perils which await the legislator when he comes to be judged by later generations. These are the words of a lawgiver who has pondered deeply over the nature and significance of his work. It would need stronger evidence than we have at our disposal to convince us that Alfred was concerned in an antiquarian revival. It is true that he expresses some hesitation in adding his own innovations—but nevertheless, he *does* innovate when necessary. Then, too, we must remember that the glory of Alfred's fame is so great that it reaches us through the dust of battle and conflict, and that to him and to his contemporaries it must have seemed that the days were very evil.

The days through which Alfred lived and fought were also the days in which he framed his laws. There was no doubt plenty of discouragement and much danger. When at last some sort of peace made it possible to think of collecting the shattered fragments of society and of endowing them once more with law, Alfred undertook a formidable task. His most significant achievement in this direction had been the re-establishment of the traditional place of the Church, and its clergy as learned men who were to afford, in the secular sphere, that light and leading which the times so sorely needed. Under such influences it was but natural that his thoughts should turn to the Mosaic laws, the golden rule, and the canons of the first Christian council which met in Jerusalem. These are all examples of terse, peremptory legislation; but above all, of legislation whose origin was explicitly stated to be divine.

They were, moreover, to be regarded as examples for the future and not merely as relics of the past. Having reproduced these passages in his introduction, he proceeds to the main business in hand: his own laws. For a century since the death of Ine there had been no legislation in England. Alfred tells us of his examination of the laws of Æthelberht of Kent, of Ine of Wessex, and of Offa of Mercia; many he retained, but others, he tells us openly, he abrogated with the advice of his wise men. He resisted the temptation (if indeed he ever felt the temptation) to re-enact, or give statutory authority to, the passages from Scripture which he reproduces in his introduction, whether they be from the Old or the New Testament. The bizarre (or indeed the disastrous) results which might follow such a course can be easily seen from the *Law and Liberties of Massachusetts*[1] which had adopted a number of passages from different books of the Old Testament before the middle of the seventeenth century, and from the Act of the Scottish Parliament dated 1567 c. 15 which like our own of 1540

[1] See the type-facsimile (1929) edited by Max Farrand of the unique edition of 1648.

(32 Henry VIII, c. 38) was taken to have the effect of making the twentieth chapter of Leviticus statute law. If Alfred had wanted to copy out ancient Semitic law he knew perfectly well where to find it; instead, he treated the Old Testament material in his introduction as justification, in a broad sense, for what he really intended to do: to legislate.

It seems highly unlikely that a monarch with so clear a conception of the urgent need for a king to legislate should be carried away with thoughts of a romantic revival of antique law, be it Semitic, Kentish, Mercian, or that of Wessex. If he enacted a tariff for personal injuries it must have been because he deemed it consonant with the times, in tune with the feelings at that moment of his people. It therefore seems safest to regard King Alfred as legislating where he could, but as restoring and adding force to those long-established institutions of his people which had proved their worth by surviving the long ordeal of the Danish wars.

The survival of long tariffs of compositions for various sorts of injury, although our earliest surviving example is in the laws of Æthelberht, is still conspicuous three hundred years later in the laws of Alfred, and can be discerned even later still. Clearly, it was deeply rooted in the country's legal customs. At this distance of time it certainly looks bizarre to find long lists of injuries equated with corresponding sums of money in the manner which has already been illustrated; this tendency to express criminal law in terms of money becomes even more remarkable when we place it beside other institutions of the age.

First there is the *wergeld* which is met at every turn in the Anglo-Saxon laws. It was primarily a sum of money due to the kindred when a man was slain, and its principal function was to express the social status of the victim; from his 'price' it was immediately apparent whether he was bond or free, noble or simple, clerk or lay. There were also notable peculiarities in different parts of the country, different coinage systems, and varying numbers of pennies to a shilling. When difficulties such as these have been taken into account, a study of the *wergeld* system gives a remarkable picture of the structure of Anglo-Saxon society. The fact that differences had to be expressed in figures compelled writers to think clearly, make up their minds, and express themselves accurately. It may be not too fanciful to think that in some remote age there may be an inquirer fortunate enough to find a table of 'income groups', and skilful enough to attempt a reconstruction of our social system from it. If such there be, he can doubtless learn much from a census return or a tax-roll; but one thing is indispensable, namely a sound understanding of how his source material came into existence in the first place, and a firm grasp of what its compilers meant it to be. On some, but not all, of these problems it is possible to venture an opinion. Besides the general (and fundamental) significance of the *wergeld*, it was of much use in calculating other payments, and was not necessarily confined to cases where a man was slain. The Anglo-Saxon laws show us some of the many uses to which it might be put. Even *bot* or compensation for injury short of death may be calculated in terms of *wergeld*, and a sum expressed as *wergeld* may be imposed upon an offender in certain circumstances; sometimes a corporal punishment, or indeed life itself, can be redeemed by payment of one's *wergeld*. Each single instance might well be susceptible of some sort of explanation, but taken all together they form a system with most disquieting features. Crime (and criminal law) was rapidly becoming a matter of money, and the various interests of aggressors, their victims, their families, their lords, their sureties, local authorities and the king himself were items in an account.

Situated as we are, in the twentieth century, it is not easy to imagine such a system at work or to form any accurate idea of its practical effect. Judging it from the standpoint of today we seem bound to observe the remarkable extent to which substance had been submerged by procedure—one might almost say that law had been lost in accountancy. Indeed, the practical business of applying the system certainly diverted men's minds to that sort of problem, and hid from them the much more fundamental question of casting into logical and orderly form the distressing phenomena associated with crime.

We can see that the existence of the system presupposes a strong family organisation; not only the offender, but his family join in raising the large sums required under Anglo-Saxon law. These sums are payable, moreover, to the family of the injured (and especially to the family of the slain) man. The practical effect of that needs careful consideration. Up to a point, it seems to betoken a group-theory of society in which the individual is almost lost. Certainly without the prompt help of the kindred it would hardly be possible to meet the heavy commitments of *wergeld*. Where (as sometimes happened) the law imposed mutilation for a misdeed, the offender could sometimes substitute a substantial payment to redeem himself, it may be even to save his life—but here again, all will depend upon having a kindred which is able and willing to help him shoulder the burden. Were they ever tempted to leave the black sheep of the family to his fate? It may well be believed that this kindred-group was able to exercise a certain amount of discipline over its members which became a valuable element in our criminal institutions. That circumstance, indeed, may have had some part in forcing men to distinguish more clearly than formerly between the tightly-knit group with its close but costly solidarity, and the undesirable individual who seemed to be a liability which the group would gladly get rid of.

To pay and receive the *wergeld* is only one aspect of the family-group; we must consider also the blood-feud. There are many grave problems which we can only mention and then set aside; 'mother-right' and 'father-right', 'spear-kin' and 'spindle-kin', the artificial gilds which seem to replace the family group on occasion, and the over-mighty family-group which sometimes became a menace by harbouring thieves and denying the king's rights.[1] There is beneath all of this the problem whether we ought to think of a *right* of carrying on a feud, and whether the function of *wer* had always been (as it later became) to preserve an offender from the effects of the blood-feud, the rule being that payment of *wer* would

---

[1] VI Æthelstan 8 § 2.

prevent the injured party from pursuing the feud. All that certainly looks as though there were a general policy against the blood-feud and attempts were being made to limit it by enforcing, as far as possible, the payment and acceptance of *wer*; when *wer* had been agreed upon, the Crown could then act vigorously against those who persisted in pursuing the blood-feud. From quite early times it is clear that the Crown realised that the blood-feud would have to be restricted: as early as the laws of Ine (just before the year 700), it was observed that a thief should not enjoy the protection of his kinsmen's feud;[1] much later, determined attempts were still being made to deal with what seemed to be an intractable problem. Towards the middle of the tenth century, King Edmund tried to separate the offender from his kin by enacting that if the kin abandon him and will not provide the *wergeld*, then the slayer should himself, alone, be subject to the vengeance of the blood-feud (as long as his kin do not harbour him with food or shelter), and that the slayer should forfeit all his property to the king.[2] Later still we find Æthelred at grips with the problem of the criminous clerk and the question of what to do when a man has two sets of rights and duties, being privileged as a priest or a monk, and being also a member of a kindred which is concerned in a blood-feud.[3] It had long been necessary (as we have seen) to make it quite clear that a thief caught in the act of thieving and killed was not entitled to the vengeance

---

[1] Ine 35; cf. II Æthelstan 20 § 7 (*c.* 927).
[2] II Edmund 1; II Edmund 7 (after 940).
[3] VIII Æthelred 23, 25 ff. (dated 1014).

of his kin, and that such a death under such circumstances did not give rise to a blood-feud.

It is a difficult matter to decide whether the considera-
tions behind this policy were really and truly derived
from thought upon the nature of crime and criminals.
As we shall see, there was anxious speculation by those
who adopted a Christian standpoint and inquired into
the nature of crime and sin. Looking at the passages
just mentioned, however, we seem to be compelled to
emphasise influences much closer to the problems of
daily life. The Anglo-Saxon laws themselves, and the
rulers who framed them, had little call to enter into
theoretical discussions or abstruse speculations; instead,
they saw all around them what seemed to be the results
of the system of blood-feud. Battle, murder and sudden
death were often the results (or could be plausibly
represented as the results) of the feud. As opinion slowly
changed, it was indeed possible to confuse the issue, as
was probably done in the minds of many people, by
reinterpreting some of the elements which composed it,
and slightly changing the emphasis to be placed upon
them: after all, was not the feud which slew a criminal
merely acting as if it were a semi-public executioner
carrying out the sentence of the law? Being local people
they were near at hand, and, being kinsmen of the slain
man, could not their diligence be relied upon? And was
not the family-group an admirable, and indeed a necessary, institution? Where nature had defaulted, it had
in fact been necessary to invent a substitute of gild-
brethren; nor were its functions confined to vengeance,
for kinsmen and gild-brethren swore as well as fought

in support of one another, and assumed heavy financial liabilities in respect of producing, when wanted, members of their group and guaranteeing their good behaviour. It seems hardly doubtful that at least part of their function was to introduce some sort of discipline into the turbulent society around them. There was something to be said for such a point of view, for it strengthened the hold of the nearest and closest society with which most men had intimate dealings, in days when kings and popes were distant and all too often ineffectual.

Finally, there is a factor of great importance which must be set beside those which have already been mentioned. Money, *wer* and *bot* had played a large part in the Anglo-Saxon criminal system, and the most summary account of it is necessarily bound to reckon with the financial element. It will be noticed that the sum assigned as *wer* is based entirely upon the status of the person concerned: he may be slave, or bond, or simple, or he may be 'dearly-born' and noble—whatever he is, the *wergeld* will mark him for life as occupying a particular station in society. Other payments may be calculated from it; sometimes a sum (being equal to the *wer*) will be imposed for some misdeed or as a compensation. In such a case it is significant that the sum to be paid will be a function of the *wer*, and its value will depend, not on the nature of the act, but upon the status of the actor, and even the tariffs of compensatory payments sometimes take note of status. It therefore follows that in some cases at least a man will pay more if he is noble or 'dearly-born', with a high *wer*, than if he were lower down in the social scale. In certain cases (but not in all) it was therefore the rule that a rich offender might have to pay more than a poor one.

Moreover, there was another side to the picture. Some men paid money; others received it. Of those who received it, some no doubt received it because their 'lordship' or other governmental rights had been infringed; but others (and it is they who interest us most at this moment) received it as *bot*—as a compensation for some injury (often a physical injury) which they had sustained. From our earliest written laws from the kingdom of Kent it is evident that we are faced with a tariff of payments which are due to one who has been injured. This simple piece of rationality was doubtless a first step only; but it was a step in the right direction. There seemed as yet no question about the rightness of this rule; if a man has been injured, he ought to be compensated, and it is the man who struck the blow who ought to be responsible for the cost. It seems sensible, and seems in tune with the Church's insistence upon satisfaction, restitution and reparation as a necessary ingredient in repentance. Indeed, in these latter days there are signs that the idea of 'restitution' and similar words (such as 'reparation'), having spent long centuries among the theologians, and later having been adopted by the lawyers (and we must not forget the politicians either), may at long last find a home in the common law. In the meantime we must lament that in the twelfth century we acquired that dangerous gift of a little learning, and so we discovered how to draw a firm line between crime and tort; as a result we awarded reparation in tort but not in crime.

It was the intrusion of the Crown into the field of public affairs, and especially the dogma that a crime was an offence against the State, that made it possible for us to unlearn a valuable lesson which a thousand years ago would never have been cast into doubt. Indeed, our earliest Anglo-Saxon laws seem innocent of what would have seemed later an elementary distinction. The *Leges Henrici Primi* were not quite ready, even yet, to make a clear-cut distinction (1114–18); it was left for Glanvill to announce dogmatically 'pleas are either criminal or civil',[1] but we may properly remember the comments of Maitland in the passage in which he draws attention to the foreign influence which guided Glanvill,[2] and to the need to 'repeat once more that every cause for a civil action is an offence, and that every cause for a civil action in the king's court is an offence against the king, punishable by amercement, if not by fine and imprisonment'. This may be driving a theory (or a definition) somewhat hard in order to maintain a paradox; one might hesitate to call a matter criminal merely because an unsuccessful demandant was 'put in mercy for his false claim'. Difficulties of this sort must be expected, however, when the categories of a foreign system are applied to a body of law such as ours, which grew up before classifications of this sort were sufficiently familiar to influence the course of its development. There is little Roman or Romanesque influence to be traced in Anglo-Saxon law, and if there were principles no one seemed to think it worth while to mention them. We must therefore

---

[1] Glanvill, lib. I, c. I.
[2] Pollock and Maitland, *History of English Law*, vol. II, p. 572.

draw our own conclusions, in default of conclusions by contemporaries whose opinion would be so much more illuminating and better informed than ours. Subject to all the perils which attend upon the discussion of so remote an age, it does seem that there were many things which we could expect to find, which the Anglo-Saxons neglected; on the other hand, we do find clear indications from the laws, early and late, that thought seemed to be fixed upon the victim and his hurt. The law felt that some sort of reparation was due to him, and the complications of the tariffs, of *bot* and *wer*—perhaps even of the blood-feud, too—were attempts to enforce that reparation where the Crown was weak and the State was not yet even a theory.

CHAPTER II

THE CROWN AND ITS RIGHTS

THE situation in which Edward I found the criminal law of this country was one of great complexity. Many ages had contributed many different elements of varying merit; indeed, while we should be ready to recognise worth wherever we find it, it will be well to bear in mind the possibility that occasionally there may be an element which was not worth much, that change is not necessarily for the better, and that reform may involve destruction as well as innovation. In our brief examination of criminal law during the Anglo-Saxon period we drew especial attention to the significance of its care for the idea of *bot*, compensation, restitution, reparation. There were other elements, however, which demand consideration. Criminal law was only one among several factors which went to make up that hard, harsh life which must have been the lot of all but a very few of the population, and we shall only form an unbalanced conception of the Anglo-Saxon law of crime if we neglect to place it among the other controls, rules, institutions and the like which together made up the society among which they lived.

It would be difficult to find anything which held a larger place in the lives of ordinary people, or indeed in the life of the nation itself, than the law and practices associated with local government. This is surely the heart of the problem of how people were governed and organised for the great tasks of war and peace before the

Conquest. To those of us who were brought up in the nineteenth-century atmosphere of constitutional history the matters which we regard as comprising that subject do indeed properly belong there; but they have other affinities too. We may well scrutinise them when we investigate the history of representation, of taxation, of military organisation, of consent generally, when it is needed in political life, of feudalism, of private jurisdiction, and much else besides; but we must not neglect them either when we are looking at criminal law. Indeed, it may be worth considering whether these institutions (especially when they were hundreds, counties and lesser courts) were not merely political assemblies, but also criminal courts.

This association of criminal enforcement with the organs of local government, and thence with the framework of national government as well, had the effect of linking together criminal law and one of the major issues of constitutional history. Maitland expressed the issue in the form in which it is now most generally known: that the later Ango-Saxon kings, especially Cnut and Edward the Confessor, the latter with 'reckless liberality', had made grants to the owners of great franchises ('immunists' he calls them) and had dilapidated the Crown and had alienated its hard-won list—already sadly short—of those royal pleas which ought to have been the kernel of a growing royal jurisdiction; not until the revolution which Henry II started had been successfully carried out was this damage repaired:[1] Maitland's study of Domesday suggested that 'the state has been very

[1] Maitland, *Domesday Book and Beyond*, pp. 282–3.

weak; the national scheme of justice has been torn to shreds by free contract, that men have had the utmost difficulty in distinguishing between property and political power, between personal relationships and the magistracy to which land is subject'.[1] In his view the men who ruled England in the age before the Conquest were not far-sighted. 'Their work ended in a stupendous failure.'[2] The work of Henry II was to put new law and new ideas in place of the old: 'it is the reconstruction of criminal justice in Henry II's time, the new learning of felonies, the introduction of the novel and royal procedure of indictment, that reduce the immunist's powers and leave him with nothing better than an unintelligible list of obsolete words'.[3]

This interpretation of the Anglo-Saxon age, and especially of the policy of Cnut and Edward the Confessor, has not been left to pass without question. There was the immediate challenge by Tait in the *English Historical Review* of 1897;[4] twenty years ago Julius Goebel began his remarkable *Felony and Misdemeanor*[5] (1937); in 1957 Helen Cam produced her very original study on 'The evolution of the mediaeval English franchise' which is to be found in the *Schweizer Beiträge zur Allgemeinen Geschichte*. Miss Cam's summary of her case against the Maitland view can be briefly put in her own words in that article:

As against Maitland's brilliant picture of decadence and feebleness, of the abandonment of powers and duties by the

---

[1] *Domesday Book and Beyond*, p. 101. [2] *Ibid.* p. 103.
[3] *Ibid.* p. 283.
[4] *English Historical Review*, vol. XII, pp. 768–77 at 772.
[5] New York, Commonwealth Fund; London, Oxford University Press.

pre-Conquest kings and the weakening of those great seignorial jurisdictions by the Angevin kings, I wish to maintain,
firstly, that no such liberties as he posits existed before the
Norman Conquest; secondly that the grants of kings were
not a sign of weakness, but rather of wisdom; and lastly that
the most extensive powers of the thirteenth century franchises
were acquired *after* the Norman Conquest as a result of the
policy of the Norman and Angevin rulers.[1]

There are the makings of a first-class debate there; but
it is not necessary for our present purpose to join it—still
less to hazard a solution. It will be enough if we bear in
mind that our concern with the enforcement of criminal
law will compel us to remember that some great matters
are involved, and that the whole fabric of government
may be at issue when we discuss criminal procedure.
Indeed, much of the domestic policy of kings such as
Cnut and Edward the Confessor turned upon their
attitude to the persistent problem of the criminal, and
most of what we know about local institutions is, in fact,
concerned with their activities in the ancient but peren-
nial task of catching thieves; if we try to picture them as
deliberating on policy or levying rates, we shall gravely
misrepresent them and mistake their place in the framework of government. Especially, too, it is essential to
remember that the king of Anglo-Saxon times was not
the omnipotent State of our own day.

We have already spoken of *bot* and *wer* and of their
place in the system of criminal law; there are other
expressions for payments due to the king, and when we
inquire into the place of the Crown in Anglo-Saxon

---

[1] *Schweizer Beiträge*, vol. xv, pp. 174–5.

criminal procedure some light may be gathered from the payments which the Crown ventured to exact.

Like any considerable subject, the king exercised a variety of rights, and the general pattern of those rights seems to be the same whether they are exercised by the king or a subject. When we find a difference it is usually a higher payment, but otherwise there is nothing to distinguish the king from his subjects. Thus we learn from the earliest extant laws of King Æthelberht that if an offence is committed while the king is feasting in a man's house double compensation is payable.[1] From the same early source (and there are many later ones) we hear of the payments due for the breach of the king's *mund*[2] and of the *mund* of many others as well.[3] Likewise in the laws of Æthelberht we hear of the king enjoying 'seignorial rights' such as some of his subjects held,[4] while from the same body of laws we learn the significant fact that one who robs the king shall pay back ninefold;[5] one who robs a bishop, however, should restore elevenfold.[6] In this table, in fact, the king shares the ninefold restitution with the simple priest—a place of honour, no doubt, but not what one would expect of a sovereign as the later Middle Ages conceived him.

There are, nevertheless, some payments which seem peculiar to the king, arising out of matters which concern his position, and not merely shared with other lords and landowners. This difference in kind, rather than in degree, is conspicuous in the best-known example of it,

---

[1] Æthelberht 3.
[2] *Ibid*. 8.
[3] *Ibid*. 15.
[4] *Ibid*. 6.
[5] *Ibid*. 4.
[6] *Ibid*. 1.

which in the Anglo-Saxon laws is described as *wite*. It occurs as early as c. 9 in the laws of Æthelberht, where we learn incidentally that it is not yet the end of the matter when a thief repays multifold the value which the law exacts; after that has been done, 'the king shall take the fine (*wite*)'. Already, then, very soon after the year 600, the Crown was exacting a payment in respect of at least one crime, which was not directed against the king himself, nor against a courtier or servant in whom the king was specially interested, as his messenger or his skilled tradesman, but against a 'freeman' generally.

As this occurs in the earliest of all our codes, that of Æthelberht, and as there is nothing to suggest that Æthelberht was putting forward a novelty of foreign origin, we seem bound to conclude that the Anglo-Saxons had no difficulty in thinking about the king exacting a *wite* in proper circumstances. It might indeed be desirable to clarify or change those circumstances from time to time, but we have no grounds for supposing that it was as yet a recent novelty if the king claimed a *wite* although neither he nor his had suffered from a crime. Especially we should beware of seeing in this any sort of Roman influence, or any temptation for our kings to equate themselves with 'the State' or 'the prince' and to regard some acts as 'crimes', and all 'crimes' as offences against the king.

By the year 695 the laws of Wihtred, king of Kent, show us that that monarch had discovered that his right to receive *wite* could be alienated; worse still, he used it to stimulate the common informer by giving him one-half of the *wite* incurred by one who had done work on a Sunday;[1] this unholy alliance of the common informer and sabbatarian legislation was to last in England another twelve and a half centuries until 1951.[2]

If we speak of Wihtred of Kent, we must necessarily speak also of his contemporary Ine of Wessex, for it is known that some communication between the neighbouring courts must have taken place. From Ine's laws it is already clear that large fines might become due,[3] and might perhaps be due to others as well as to the king, when a crime (especially one of violence) had been committed in the recipient's house or on his land. There are other cases too where complicated little calculations might have to be carried out before it was quite certain how much money had to be paid.[4] Thus a man who captured a thief was supposed to give him up to the king and get ten shillings (it is not said where the money comes from, but possibly it is provided by the king). But if the thief escapes, the captor must pay a *wite* (no doubt to the king); moreover, if the captor wishes to clear himself from the suspicion of being concerned in the escape he must take an oath equal to the value of the stolen goods plus the fine.[5] A somewhat similar use of the fine if a man has failed to 'free himself from the fine' by satisfactorily performing an oath is to be found at a later passage in the same laws.[6]

A century later the laws of Alfred show how complica-

---

[1] Wihtred 11.

[2] Common Informers Act (1951). Cf. G. R. Elton, 'Informing for profit: a sidelight on Tudor methods of law-enforcement', *Cambridge Historical Journal*, vol. XI (1954), p. 149.

[3] Ine 6. [4] Ine 76.
[5] Ine 28. [6] Ine 54.

tions had grown. When a culprit's hand was ordered to be struck off because he had committed a theft with it, he might nevertheless redeem it (if the authorities permit) by a payment according to his *wer*—although no name for it is specified, some sort of fine is clearly indicated.[1] Indeed, it was considered necessary to introduce some order into a tangled situation, for Alfred sets up a very rough calculus for fines based upon the value of the goods stolen, and abolishes the differences in those fines which were based upon the nature (and not the value) of the things stolen—he expressly mentions gold, horses and bees.[2] The lender of a weapon used to kill a man is expected to contribute one-third of the fine;[3] moreover, it is clear that sometimes, at least, the *wite* was payable to others than the king—an alderman, for example.[4]

In the laws of Æthelstan, a generation after Alfred's death, the payment of penal sums to the king becomes clearly stated and enjoined in the laws. Thus, one who aids a thief must pay a fine of 120s. to the king,[5] and if the thief himself is put in prison he must serve forty days, and if he wants to get out and be released to sureties he he must pay 120s. (again, to the king, no doubt).[6] Again, a lord who refuses justice and sides with one of his dependants will also have to pay 120s.[7] The same code of laws elaborates a number of instances when the king will have his *oferhiernes*, the heavy fine of 120s. for insubordination (as it is generally translated). As the provisions for this fine become more frequent and more

---

[1] Alfred 6 § 1. [2] Alfred 9 §§ 1, 2.
[3] Alfred 19 § 1. [4] Alfred 38.
[5] II Æthelstan 1 § 5. [6] II Æthelstan 1 § 3.
[7] II Æthelstan 3.

33

widespread, it is clear that the power of the Crown (at least in terms of money) is becoming more extensive, and that flagrant failure to do right is an offence which the Crown will punish heavily, even although it did not figure in the older laws, and even although the king is neither victim, nor the victim's lord or employer. His sole interest in the matter, and his sole title to exact payments in respect of it, is derived from his position as king.

All the same, whatever the pretensions of the king might be, there were others who also had their claims, and (in theory at least) those claims ought to be met. The bill was long and complicated, and Maitland endeavoured to show the nature of our oldest criminal law by constructing an imaginary example, having first warned us that different parts of the country would have materially different rules on a number of points. Placing himself at the middle years of Henry I,

let us suppose [he wrote] that a man learned in the law is asked to advise upon a case of homicide. Godwin and Roger met and quarrelled, and Godwin slew Roger. What must be paid; by whom? to whom? Our jurist is not very careful about those psychical elements of the case which might interest us, but on the other hand he requires information about a vast number of particulars which would seem to us trivial. He cannot begin to cast up his sum until he has before him some such statement as this: Godwin was a free ceorl of the Abbot of Ely; Roger, the son of a Norman father, was born in England of an English mother and was a vavassor of Count Alan: the deed was done on the Monday after Septuagesima, in the county of Cambridge, on a road which ran between the land which Gerard, a Norman knight, held of count Eustace, and the land of the bishop of Lincoln: this

road was not one of the king's highways: Godwin was pursued
by the neighbours into the county of Huntingdon and
arrested on the land of the Abbot of Ramsey: Roger, when
the encounter took place, was on his way to the hundred
moot: he has left a widow, a paternal uncle and a maternal
aunt. As a matter of fact, the result will probably be that
Godwin, unable to satisfy the various claims to which his
deed has given rise, will be hanged or mutilated. This, however, is but a slovenly, practical solution of the nice problem,
and even if he be hanged, there may be a severe struggle over
such poor chattels as he had.[1]

Maitland here assembled a goodly number of those legal
problems which were inherent in the Anglo-Saxon legal
system. Before we pass judgement on such a system, it is
well to think for a moment of the grounds upon which we
would criticise it. That it was technical is hardly a cause
for reproof. Our law became much more technical than
that, as it became more extensive and precise. It has
always seemed to me that technicality is a virtue in law,
as in any other field of scholarship. In the first place, it
makes for brevity, and in the second place it imposes
accuracy—each of them a virtue of the highest importance. But before everything else, it is necessary to
direct the finest and most accurate of our tools towards
the problems which lie nearest the heart of the matter.
It is plain from a perusal of the Anglo-Saxon laws that a
case of homicide raised, in fact, those very questions
which Maitland embodied in the passage just quoted;
the general framework of the legal points was the
question 'How much?' That one question serves all

[1] Pollock and Maitland, *History of English Law*, vol. I, pp. 106–7. This is
a rich (but not entirely exhaustive) list of puzzles such as must have often
occurred in practice.

purposes, be they the damage to injured parties, the sums payable to the dead man's kin, the penalties to his lord, to the landowners of the localities involved, and the rights of the Crown.

It is clear to us now that such a single formula is too narrow to contain matters which now seem to us related, perhaps, but fundamentally disparate. As late as the eleventh century it was still possible, perhaps, to regard the questions which Maitland put to his imaginary lawyer as being of primary importance to that sort of case, but the time was to come (as yet a distant time, no doubt) when crime and tort, the sovereignty of the king, and the rights of various landlords, would be seen to differ, not only in degree, but in kind. It would only then be possible to discard many of the queries which Maitland enumerated, and to concentrate upon matters which today seem more truly fundamental.

It is those fundamental matters which separate us from other ages. The seventeenth century, which had begun to see the significance of a 'fair trial' as a constitutional safeguard (especially in the matter of treason and the statute of 1696),[1] the eighteenth century with its insistence on strict legality, the nineteenth century with its interest in criminology, the twentieth century with its insistence upon psychology, have each of them suggested different matters as being the foundations upon which criminal law is constructed. It is not necessary to believe that any of them had got to the root of things, although we may well admit that they all of them made contribu-

[1] S. Rezneck, 'The statute of 1696', *Journal of Modern History*, vol. II, pp. 5–26.

tions which carried the discussion a little further. Certainly the Anglo-Saxon age had devised a rough and ready calculus for expressing at least some of the factors in the situation of criminal law. In one sense, their calculus was admirable; it had the merit of that precision which figures always have for those who think (or more often assume) that they can be added, subtracted, multiplied and divided, and somehow still produce results of general value. As we watch Maitland's imaginary lawyer casting up his account, we can see from the surviving Anglo-Saxon laws where he would have to look in order to find the correct figures to fill in; but we can also see that many of the figures which he will have to supply relate to things which the keener analysis of later ages will recognise as not truly commensurable.

But one thing had been done: criminal enforcement and compensation for crime, *wite* and *bot* and the various royal and seignorial dues had been systematised in terms of money. Some of it was payable to the king, but much more of it was due to various private persons or to various lords—as yet, not necessarily great lords by any means. At the end of the Anglo-Saxon age we find those payments very often in the hands of magnates of various sorts—principally the great monastic houses. In a number of cases we seem to see how they got there, when we find that an Anglo-Saxon charter purports to grant these rights from the Crown to a church.

We are thus brought face to face with the problem with which this chapter began: the fragmentation of public authority in the last years of the Anglo-Saxon age, especially in the reigns of Cnut and Edward the

Confessor. The classical exposition of that critical but puzzling theory looks especially at the eventual result, namely the abandonment by the Crown of various sources of revenue into the hands of great landowners; did not this betoken the avarice of the monasteries, and the weakness—perhaps I should say, 'weak-mindedness'—of the kings who seemed to be concerned mainly with their own soul's health? Anyhow, there are occasional effects of that policy upon local government which subsist to this day and which may, no doubt, adorn a tale, even although they point their moral a little ambiguously. But there is another point of view which we may well consider. The word 'feudalism' is familiar enough, and comforting enough, to provide facile explanations which we hastily accept because they seem, at least on paper, to dispose of our problems. Nineteenth-century liberalism has left it in as evil a posture as did eighteenth-century republicanism. The bold, bad barons (it was said) had pulled down the monarchy in the interests of 'feudal anarchy'; these same magnates, moreover, who long before had established the noble families and the idea of '*noblesse*' throughout Europe, had already destroyed the relics of primeval Germanic democracy, traces of which still subsisted (it was thought) in the system of English local government.

Familiar as are these two possibilities, we shall possibly get nearer to the truth if we try and see the situation as it appeared to contemporaries. To them, we may perhaps conjecture, the problem was not the political theory of the monarchy, nor the democratic theory of local government, but the practical, ever-pressing problem of criminal law enforcement. It may be presumed that it was from this point of view that Miss Cam has suggested that the Anglo-Saxon kings, especially Cnut and Edward the Confessor (who have suffered heavily at the hands of constitutional historians), had all the time been keeping their eye on the ball, and (if my gloss on her theory is acceptable) that they had realised that the fundamental problem of their day was the difficulty of enforcing the merest elements of peace and order in the country. Cnut referred several times to the activities of devils in the land,[1] and three centuries earlier King Wihtred had expressed concern at the extent of devil-worship in the country;[2] even later than the day of Cnut, the great canonist Ivo of Chartres gave in his *Decretum*[3] an astonishing list of 'superstitions', as he calls them, which were still rampant at the end of the eleventh century in the French countryside. (The wickedness of giving presents on New Year's Day is one of the more innocent of them.[4]) When we read our chronicles we must remember that they came from monasteries which were centres of enlightenment in lands which all around them were fundamentally heathen, and that Christianity as a religion, and the ethic which it contained, was as yet only imperfectly apprehended by the *pagani*, the *paysans*, the countrymen, the pagans, who constituted the great mass of the population.

[1] I Cnut 4 § 2; I Cnut 26 § 2.

[2] Wihtred 12, 13.

[3] Ivo of Chartres, *Decretum*, pars xi (in Migne, *Patrologia Latina*, CLXI, 746 ff.).

[4] On this practice in England, see G. R. Owst, '*Sortilegium* in English homiletic literature', *Studies Presented to Sir Hilary Jenkinson* (1957), pp. 272–303, at p. 276.

That was the situation which confronted our Anglo-Saxon kings—even the later of them: the urgent need of the hour was to catch and dispose of thieves and murderers. The means at their disposal were woefully slight; the only way of sending a writ was for a man to get on a horse and carry it, perhaps a considerable distance through probably unfriendly country—a costly, slow and perhaps perilous enterprise. To try and impose law and order by such means, directed and controlled from the centre of government (wherever that happened to be at the moment), was clearly hopeless. Catching criminals was essentially a local matter, which could only be effectually carried out by a man on the spot.

The only local power which seemed to offer any hope of enforcing criminal law was the local magnate. The imposing experiment of the great earls who 'played politics' and ruined (or at any rate did not save) the Anglo-Saxon state, is one example of the perils which beset the last kings of the House of Wessex. It must long have been clear that the monasteries were the only hope. It was within their walls that there lived a community which could take a larger view of life than some of its neighbours, and which to some extent at least transmitted a part of that spirit and respect for learning which became one of the glories of the Benedictine order. If the ideas of law and order had anywhere survived the Danish invasions, it was in the great monastic houses, renewed as they often were by the transplantation of monks who originated from, or had received some of their training from, continental establishments. Equally important was the fact that the great monastic house had perforce to give some heed to the duties involved in being the landlord of wide estates, and this necessarily meant rather more than mere agricultural estate management. It would hardly be possible for a monastery to conduct even its temporal affairs without exerting some influence upon those who exploited its lands, and its officers in the natural course of their duties must have gained a fair knowledge of what was going on in the countryside.

Already such houses had some of the financial advantages of criminal enforcement, simply because they were (and for long had been) the lords of certain men, or of certain lands. Here were elements which were conspicuous in the growth of feudalism throughout the west. They were, moreover, native and natural products of local conditions. The wider and more general question of feudalism is much too big to be treated here; but we are bound to be concerned with the more immediate question of the feudalisation of criminal institutions in England. The long, slow movement which thrust criminal law into the hands, eventually, of the Crown has left us with the impression that the Crown in older times must have been improvident or careless to part with it and to allow the feudatories to exercise it. The long line of charters which actually show the Crown granting this jurisdiction (or parts of it) to individual subjects, especially churches, seemed clear proof to the contemporaries of Stubbs and Maitland that the Crown was frittering away a precious heritage for reasons which historians could not approve or, indeed, understand. The intrusion of the feudal spirit into criminal jurisdiction seemed an unqualified disaster.

The alternative interpretation which Miss Cam has suggested will relieve us, I think, of some of the difficulties inherent in the older view. The barest outline of it has already been mentioned;[1] at various other points of that paper on the evolution of the franchise there will be found indications of where the argument will lead us. Thus we find the important observation that 'there is no reference in any genuine charter to the exclusion of royal agents from the privileged lands until after the Norman Conquest'.[2] This is true (or very nearly so).[3] After the Conquest, moreover, the lords of liberties undoubtedly received much larger powers, and more precise recognition, as Norman and Angevin kings fashioned the great palatinates which were taking shape at that moment. Was it, then, the vigorous and able kings from William the Conqueror to John, who had been more reckless than their Anglo-Saxon forbears in dilapidating the patrimony of the Crown? Miss Cam would save us from so unlikely a conclusion by suggesting that we confuse the issue if we state it in terms of subtractions from a once omnipotent monarchy.

The franchise...is part of the royal scheme of government. Edward I, in his nationwide enquiry into his subjects' title to the liberties they held and into the manner in which they exercised them, had no intention of eliminating the franchises; he would not have found it easy to staff an alternative royal system. They made a real contribution to the work

[1] Above, pp. 28–9.

[2] H. M. Cam, *op. cit.* p. 176; cf. F. E. Harmer, *Anglo-Saxon Writs*, pp. 127–8 and Julius Goebel, *Felony and Misdemeanor*, p. 255.

[3] See F. E. Harmer, *Anglo-Saxon Writs*, pp. 128, 171 and writ no. 28 (p. 183) for a possible exception.

of governing the kingdom, and many of the franchise-holders were proud of that contribution, even though it entailed 'great and continuous labour' as one of them called it.[1]

The policy of Edward I towards the franchises, as towards feudalism generally, was not to destroy but to fulfil. Feudalism was part of the pattern of society and neither he nor anyone else propounded a 'brave new world' as an alternative to it. His policy was not to re-fashion the framework of government, but to get better results, if that could be done, from the machinery with which he and his people had been familiar for genera-tions. He and they, for centuries, had known the local notable (whether lay or ecclesiastical) and had acqui-esced in his position, both as expressed in his rough-and-ready rule over his estates and the countryside generally, and also as implying that the exercise of power brought with it corresponding duties and responsibilities. To the inhabitants he was (or ought to be) a terror to evil-doers, and a protector to the poor and the law-abiding; to the king he was conspicuous as a man active in local affairs, who was constantly in demand for all sorts of duties on juries, assizes, commissions and the like, and if he were the head of an ecclesiastical corporation there might be endless work which he could usefully do at the centre as well as locally. Wealthy persons and corpora-tions were willing to incur considerable expense in order to take their part in the thankless but necessary work of local government. In the later Middle Ages it was Parliament and the commission of the peace which were

[1] H. M. Cam, *op. cit.* p. 181.

most generally the formal institutions through which such men worked; indeed, for a time both members of Parliament and justices of the peace were paid, for they had to travel far and devote much time to the costly demands of royal government. Much earlier, in the Anglo-Saxon age, it was to men of this type that Cnut and Edward the Confessor had recourse when the stern duty of pursuing thieves and suppressing disorder needed the strong right arm of the local notable who should be above all, on the spot, with local knowledge, with time to spare and with stewards, bailiffs, servants and followers who could be called upon in emergency. For centuries the law had been calling upon all honest men to get themselves 'lordship' with men of substance who would accept a certain responsibility for them and their behaviour; the general principle that criminal law enforcement should make great use of those who were powerful enough to play their part in it, had long been unquestioned. The Anglo-Saxon laws had not neglected, furthermore, to recognise the large financial interest which the lords of men, and of places, could properly enjoy when their peace and protection were infringed. There was no possibility of the kings' maintaining an effective organisation for law enforcement: but they could, and did, when the old financial system broke down, patch up the fragments, and even transfer to some of the lords a portion of the revenues which the king had succeeded in acquiring. The policies which seemed to the older historians an abandonment of the Crown's duties in criminal law enforcement, and as endowing the great ecclesiastical and lay feudatories with the profits, will therefore appear, on re-examination, as susceptible of an interpretation which is more consonant with contemporary practices, and which makes it clear that the problem before our kings was to find out the most effective type of machinery for law enforcement.

At the moment, it seemed as if this movement towards feudalism was triumphant, in criminal law as well as in property and military affairs, and that the feudalisation of criminal justice offered the most promising line of attack upon the perpetual problem of criminal law and its enforcement. That may well have been the case; but it was not the whole case by any means, and we should remember that an exact uniformity over the whole land did not yet exist. Local variants may well have been numerous, and may have been sometimes of serious importance. At the most crucial moment of this history, the anonymous author of the book called *Leges Henrici Primi*[1] was making his gallant attempt to state the law around him. The mystery—at times the incoherence—which so strikingly marks this work, will remind us that the writer was living at the height of a crisis in English law. He was undoubtedly trying to be useful and to help his fellow lawyers—if we should use such a word about the years 1114–18—when he was composing his tract. He certainly was not a mere antiquarian with no interest in the contemporary scene. Indeed, it would seem that he was not at all sure which way to turn, or where to look for his law. The Anglo-Saxon laws he studied carefully (for it must have been the same man who had translated

[1] Text in F. Liebermann, *Gesetze der Angelsachsen* (Halle, 1898–1916), vol. I, pp. 545 ff.; B. Thorpe, *Ancient Laws and Institutes*, vol. I, pp. 497 ff.

them into Latin in *Quadripartitus*); his knowledge of, and
dependence upon them is certainly shown in the *Leges
Henrici Primi*. His appreciation of the work of Cnut is
well attested; but he gave the place of honour to
Henry I's Coronation Charter and in breathless confusion he mingled the feudalism of that document with
the more ancient texts of Cnut and others. He would
have us believe that these old laws and practices were
just as much current law as were the most recent feudal
dispositions in Henry I's charter. There seems to be no
way of avoiding the conclusion that he was writing at the
critical moment when the old was yielding place to the
new. He tells us about the county, the hundred and the
like; he still talks about *bot* and *wer*; he warns us at the
outset that Wessex, Mercia and the Danelaw have distinct
bodies of law, and familiarly uses the old Anglo-Saxon
laws, especially those of Cnut from which he draws the
famous words of c. 10 *De iure Regis*, which are familiar to
every reader of Stubbs's *Charters*.[1] The author puts these
'royal rights' in very interesting company, for he first
tells us of 'the general pleas of the counties' (c. 7), then
of 'hundreds' (c. 7, §8, c. 8), some generalities about
causes (c. 9); then follows this list of 'royal rights' (c. 10)
and then he tells us of 'church pleas pertaining to the
king' (c. 11), of 'emendable pleas' (c. 12), of 'pleas
which put one in the king's mercy' (c. 13)—and so on,
through pell-mell discussions of 'reliefs' (a thoroughly
feudal expression) (c. 14), Danegeld (c. 15), forests
(c. 16), *sac* and *soc*, and much else besides. It all illustrates the deep confusion caused by the co-existence of

[1] Stubbs, *Select Charters* (9th ed.), p. 125.

the old and the new—of the old Saxon and the new feudal. The author of the *Leges* gives us this formidable mixture of laws just as he found it; only the sketchiest attempt at arrangement reveals the author's presence or his individual efforts. Nevertheless, we can see what had been happening. To begin with, the three bodies of law, Wessex, Mercia and the Danelaw, although differing in detail, are now all under one king who enjoys the royal rights allowed under each law. The author tells us of *sac* and *soc*, *tol* and *team*, and the other ancient jingles of Anglo-Saxon law. He wrote in Latin (or something like it) and he was already able to use words which became classical in the later common law as technical terms: we thus hear of *forisfactura* or '*forfeiture*' and of *misericordia*, the 'mercy' of the king or of a lord which accepts a money payment in lieu of some heavier punishment, and which has affinities with the 'amercement' in common law courts on the one hand, and with the idea of 'mercy' as a virtue in the theological sense on the other. Above all, and at the front of his book, he put the Coronation Charter of Henry I. Much as he was impressed by the Anglo-Saxon law (and especially that of Cnut), he seems to have been deeply aware of the preponderant position of the Crown. Unmistakably, he must be classed as a 'royalist', looking to the Crown for the direction and development of the criminal law in England. The creation and enlargement of 'franchises' seems to him to be a natural, and indeed a useful, development in the eternal and basic duty of maintaining public peace and order. Nevertheless, he who well knew of the feud of Empire and Papacy, of the

47

Regnum and the *Sacerdotium*, makes no attempt to present the material which he was studying as a struggle of the Old English and New Norman, or of King against Feudalism, even although he was assuredly no stranger to the conflict of ideas, and approved of what he saw going on around him.[1]

If he had returned to the scene about two generations later our author would have seen the direction of events even more plainly. Where Henry I had merely picked up the fragments of Anglo-Saxon law, stray memories of Imperial and Roman grandeur, and the growing and spreading notions which were to give form to feudalism, Henry II had combined them into a compact whole. Instead of indefinite and even antique 'rights', the king was now furnished with 'pleas of the Crown' which were not merely 'rights' which he happened to hold (as many other men held rights of various sorts), but were attributes of his crown; being a king necessarily implied the jurisdiction of pleas of the Crown. That 'tremendous *imperium* of royal majesty' which the author of the *Leges Henrici Primi* spoke about so solemnly,[2] was now something much more than words with an antique ring; Henry II had filled them with substance. From feudalism 'theft' and 'man-slaying' got a newer and more hateful name: *felony*.

Above all, Henry II had thought hard about the problems of procedure, and had entertained disquieting

---

[1] Such distinctions could be provoked, however, by the harshness of the forest laws; and the idealisation of Edward the Confessor did lead to the *Constitutiones Cnuti* (printed by Liebermann, vol. I, pp. 620 ff. as *Pseudo-Cnut de Foresta*, the *Leges Edwardi Confessoris* (in Liebermann, vol. I, pp. 627 ff.) and other forgeries.   [2] *Leges Henrici Primi*, c. VI.

thoughts about the puzzling matter of proof. The dependence of the Anglo-Saxon system (and indeed of the 'appeal of felony' in the Norman age) upon an individual accuser coming forward, ready to 'follow the trail' and to keep in motion a complicated system of procedure (apparently at his own expense) was a serious defect; and it can hardly be considered as much of an improvement when after the Conquest the accuser in an appeal of felony was required to appear fully armed and to engage in single combat with the accused. Under such conditions we need feel no surprise that there was a general reluctance to commence criminal proceedings. The device applied by Henry II was to compel local communities to 'present', or report, to the authorities those in their area who were suspected of the most grave offences—felony. As always, the problem of making an accusation was primarily a local one, and the presentment (or, as the case might be, the indictment)[1] was necessarily made by a 'grand jury' of the locality concerned; the official who took it might be some minor officer of a hundred, or the sheriff, or a justice of the king; but one thing is abundantly clear—it is a royal procedure, and the Crown and its officers are in command at every stage. The presentment or indictment being made, the accused is to be held for trial, and royal justices will be commissioned in due course to 'deliver the gaol' of such prisoners. Out of the confusion of new and old, which so sorely tried the anonymous writer of the *Leges Henrici Primi*, there had come some sort of

[1] For the technical distinction between presentment and indictment, see Blackstone, *Commentaries* (1765), vol. IV, p. 301.

order. He was to be the last writer on our criminal law who would have to deal with the ancient tariffs and the 'rights' with their uncouth names, which families, employers, lords and even kings could claim. The complicated bills could be left for the curiosity of a Maitland to elucidate. For the first time, some sort of clarity and order could be discerned in our criminal law. But it was the Crown which put it there.

CHAPTER III

THE CRIMINAL AND INTENTION

IT would be useless to pretend that life is simple, or that the course of history could be described as a development in one straight line from a single point of origin. We should flatter ourselves, moreover, if we too lightly assumed that all our decisions were rational, and that our own lives, and those of our ancestors, were straightforward exercises in logical deduction, and nothing more. While it is true, as we have already seen, that the Anglo-Saxon laws of the various peoples settled in England are essentially primitive, unorganised, and do not reveal any sustained and ordered thought upon crime or its problems, nevertheless we can see that there were movements, conflicts even, which must be weighed carefully if we are to present an intelligible view of this history. The various Anglo-Saxon laws had at least the elements from which to weave a system; *wer* and *bot* and *wite* had meanings and a usefulness which they do not explain to us—still less do they give us any critical thoughts upon them—and so we are left to discover, with very little aid from contemporaries, the fundamental ideas which lay at the root of their criminal law. All the same, there were some that seem to be fairly evident. *Wer* is clearly a social element, primarily indicative of the rank of a man and of the sum of money which his kindred could claim if he is slain. *Bot* is a form of compensation, not assessed by a judge or a jury, but pre-ordained in a tariff. If one can judge upon so delicate a matter, *wite* seems to have, at least upon some occasions, punitive implications which are much less conspicuous in the other words. All three terms, however, seem to have at their root the idea of 'compensation', and even *wite* would seem to be an attempt to provide a sort of *solatium*, so to speak, for the grave affront to the king when the more serious crimes are committed.

The fact that precise rules about these matters were almost inevitably rules about money, and the rights to claim money from various people, no doubt helped to emphasise the fact that there was a pecuniary value to lordship and to reinforce the tendency towards feudal institutions which was apparent throughout western Europe. The more immediate result was to introduce a new element into the sphere of criminal law, and its most obvious effects were the Gallicising of our legal language, both civil and criminal; by the period of Edward I, the uncouth vocabulary of the Anglo-Saxons had been replaced by technical terms of French form which are most of them with us today.

The feudalisation and Gallicisation of our law and legal language must not hide from us the most radical of all the results which were to flow from the Anglo-Saxon situation, namely the rise to supremacy of the Crown. It is hardly yet possible to speak with assurance about much of the detail of this history; of the ultimate result, however, there can be little doubt. The law of *wer* and of *bot* yielded place to the law of *wite* which the Anglo-Norman kings knew under the Gallicised expressions of 'forfeiture' (*forisfactura*) and 'amercement' (*amerciamentum*).

This development was certainly a step towards the rationalising of our criminal law; but it meant also that our Anglo-Norman kings had something more than the purely Anglo-Saxon elements of *wer* and *bot* and *wite* at their disposal. The antique air which surrounds so much Anglo-Saxon law cannot fail to puzzle the reader. We have already had to consider the doubt whether King Alfred was dealing with living law when he laid down rules about the feud and seemingly primitive notions of liability attached to weapons, about noxal surrender, and the like. These doubts are not to be confined to the laws of that monarch; it seems to be constantly hinted in the laws that they do not tell us the whole story, and one has the uneasy feeling that there is much more which ought to appear in a *History of English Criminal Law* (if there were such a book) than can be found, at least on the surface, in the Anglo-Saxon laws.

There entered into our history, in fact, a new element which had to be reckoned with by the latest of the Anglo-Saxon kings. This was the Church.

At the moment when our Anglo-Saxon laws appear, the Merovingian church was entering upon a decline; councils of bishops became infrequent and the Merovingian church disintegrated, to fall sometimes into the hands of laymen, and the collapse of the hierarchy and ecclesiastical discipline can be described by no other word than anarchy. Christendom was in fact slowly drifting apart. The east was most fruitful in theology; Rome and Italy followed their ancient vocation of law— in this case, canon law; the outskirts of Europe, which meant Ireland and to some extent England and parts of northern Europe, devoted much of their energy to moral theology, which they conceived and elaborated within the peculiar structure of the Irish church.

The structure and habits of the 'insular' churches, as they may be called, were particularly favourable to these developments. Their basic organisation was monastic, and they lacked the cities, and their accompanying bishops, which gave form and authority to the hierarchical framework of the Church in southern Europe. It was hardly to be avoided that these developments of the 'insular' churches should contrast strongly with those of the Roman tradition. In that tradition there was enshrined the culture of city-life and strong memories of the idea of law—indeed, of Roman law—with a territorial episcopate held together by fairly frequent councils of bishops intent upon maintaining authority, uniformity and order.[1] The decline of authority and organisation in the Merovingian church had left the way open for other influences; Spanish and, especially, insular. The missionary zeal of the Irish church was outstanding and its influence spread far and wide as its emissaries covered England and Europe. Other Celtic races also took part, and Bretons and Welsh joined English and Irish in producing those Penitentials which were the especial expression of the insular point of view.

A comparison of the Penitentials and the Anglo-Saxon laws shows clearly their importance, and the well-known study of T. P. Oakley[2] in the 'Columbia

[1] Paul Fournier and Gabriel Le Bras, *Histoire des collections canoniques en Occident*, vol. I (1931), pp. 50–1, 82–7.
[2] T. P. Oakley, *English Penitential Discipline and Anglo-Saxon Law in their Joint Influence* (1923), Columbia Studies, etc., no. 242.

Studies in History, Economics and Public Law' clearly illustrates their role in giving spiritual support to the endeavours of the secular powers to maintain a system of criminal law. When we consider the effectiveness of Anglo-Saxon law, or attempt to estimate its aims and policies, it is dangerous to omit the Penitentials, which made it one of their objects to go hand-in-hand with the secular law. Their attitude to the feud was highly critical. Where the secular laws regarded the slaying of a man as entirely justified if the rules of the feud had been observed, the Penitentials nevertheless imposed a heavy penance.[1] The secular laws prescribe the payment of various compositions for theft, and of course in the outstanding case where it was traditional, the payment of *wer* for a slaying. The Penitential books add valuable support when they reduce their heavy penances, *if* monetary composition had been offered and paid. Valuable aid was also afforded in those numerous cases where an oath formed part of the machinery prescribed in the laws. Perjury and false witness were heavily penalised, and the Penitentials seem determined to make the oath a matter of great moment and of real value when it is associated with transaction-witnesses, compurgation, exculpatory and decisory oaths.[2]

Needless to say, there are numerous problems surrounding the Penitentials which we should be aware of, although they do not directly impinge upon our subject. Their date and attribution (it is hardly possible to use so precise a word as authorship) and the relationship

[1] *Ibid.* p. 169.
[2] Oakley, *op. cit.* pp. 174 ff.

55

between one Penitential and another are essential at the outset before we can make any use of them at all. We then have to remember that they have an important place in the general history of penance and especially upon the different methods of public and private penance. We have then to consider the vital question of the conflict between the Roman and the insular literature on penance; though this controversy was primarily expressed in theological terms, it was something wider than the points of theology which it contained. The Penitentials, however admirable we are tempted to think they were, contained faults which would have seemed especially serious to one who had absorbed the Roman tradition. The disorder of these books, the variations and discrepancies between the various Penitentials, their serious divergence from Roman doctrine and practice at certain points, especially in the matter of marriage, their lack of authority of any sort, and their lack of uniformity among themselves, their origin in the private judgement or fancy of private persons with no official position, and generally whose name is unknown—such things are the negation of all that can be described as a Roman sense of law and order, and ill assort with the Roman conception of a hierarchically organised church, which has no place for ventures of that sort.

Those were grave defects. There were others. At first sight it would seem that a Penitential was a precise and inflexible tariff—not of money, but of periods of penance, long or short, for a large variety of crimes, great and small. As it became more commonly known that serious divergences existed, the realisation grew that there was room, indeed there might be necessity, for picking and choosing; in other words, for discretion. There was indeed a universal tendency towards laxity, and this coincided all too closely with the disintegration of church life in Merovingian France. That growing laxity and the invitation to the use of discretion is remarkably illustrated in certain extreme examples of commutation—that is to say, the substitution for the penance imposed of some other penance in its place, often to be performed by some other persons. There were men who would fast (at so much a day), and a wealthy delinquent would soon commute his penance to fasts, prayers and the like, performed by others, although at his expense.[1]

This last development of 'commutation' robbed the penitential system of much of its claim to respect, and reduced it in the end to a situation somewhat like that of the Anglo-Saxon laws: it had always been a tariff, and it was now barely disguised—it was in practice a tariff of money payments. The financial element had therefore intruded once again. Here, then, was one more serious objection to the penitential system and especially to its practice in a large part of Christendom.

Nevertheless, the very defects of the penitential literature served a useful purpose,[2] and the discrepancies and contradictions contained in the books were sufficiently startling to put their readers upon their inquiry. When

[1] Fournier and Le Bras, *Collections canoniques*, vol. I, p. 355.
[2] On the '*rôle social, et l'on peut dire: le rôle civilisateur des pénitentiels*' see the judicious summary by Fournier and Le Bras, vol. I, pp. 56–62.

the insular churches set their minds to a study of penance and of moral theology, they undertook one of the most difficult investigations which lie at the roots of law, as well as of theology. Their method was, in general, sound. Material first of all had to be collected; the arrangement of it was no doubt primitive, but in general the compilers were as scientific as they could be. They even showed a rough notion of authority when it became customary to place penitential books under the name of some famous or saintly personage—indeed, one famous collection purports to be the 'judgements', *judicia*, of Theodore, Archbishop of Canterbury. Prominent persons of the not-too-distant past may well have left traditions (as Theodore seems to have done) which appreciative followers and admirers collected and subsequently circulated. In a sense they had sought for authority, but it was the prestige of a famous name, and not the authority which, in the Roman view, should attach to the decrees of a pope or a council. The manuscript tradition of such a text presents difficulties of its own; the copying of figures (and a penitential consists largely of figures) is likely to ensnare the most conscientious scribe; to those involuntary errors must be added others of a somewhat less innocent kind, although their presence is hardly to be blamed when we consider the difficulties of the age. A scribe (or his master) may well be puzzled by what he sees in the exemplar before him, and may attempt to 'correct' it; or it may be that he flatly disapproves of what he reads, and substitutes something else which he thinks better represents the mind of the original author. More serious still, he may find something in his exemplar which seems to him erroneous, or unreasonable, or too harsh, or in some way reprehensible. He may himself suffer from what has been called a 'dangerous originality'.[1] Whatever the reason, the result will be a further corruption of the text and a growth of that increasing laxness which the manuscripts as a whole display.

The divergences of the manuscripts could not fail, to thoughtful minds, to produce an uneasy attitude towards this type of literature. The literature was urgently needed; yet it failed to give the guidance which simple and unlearned clergy needed in difficult cases. Worse still, when it did give a precise rule, it often happened that a different rule was to be found in some other collection. The problem was not merely one of ascertaining the true, or probable, text of the original work. It went much deeper than that. The fundamental questions raised by these discrepancies went to the roots of law and moral theology. This was not always seen at once.

The first part of the the question was to establish that whatever 'the book' says, the individual confessor may, and indeed must, exercise discretion. This was a step forward, in law, as it was in moral theology. There is always a temptation, which we all have felt from schooldays, to look up the answer at the end of the book. That is a simple procedure, and in normal circumstances ought to produce the right result. The very object of Penitentials was just that—to give the conclusions reached by wise and holy men, so that lesser mortals could apply the results of their wisdom to the problems

[1] The phrase comes from Fournier and Le Bras, vol. I, p. 58.

which arise in the course of clerical duties. It is a human weakness to ask for a sign, and to expect a straight answer to every question; and there is a very real temptation to rely upon the 'book'—be it Bible, Penitential, *Corpus Juris*, or a *Manual of Police Procedure*—to give a clear answer ready for use in all our difficulties. In a hurry, or in an emergency, even the *sortes Virgilianae* will perhaps help to guide us; but when there arise difficulties in which even the books fail us (and they often do), something more fundamental must be brought into the account. The discrepancies of the Penitentials could only have the effect of presenting the reader with a choice, and with throwing upon him the serious burden of examining the whole question and of making that choice. He must use his brains and not rely too implicitly upon what he finds in whatever book he happens to possess, or chooses to possess. Even the Penitentials themselves sometimes openly allow a confessor to use his discretion. Certainly it became general teaching that laws and Penitentials alike are insufficient if they merely contain tariffs of penalties, and we must bear in mind, when we read the Anglo-Saxon laws, the fact that they may not have been as rigid in practice as they seem, and that (at least at the close of the Anglo-Saxon period) the laws themselves contain passages which make it clear that they were not to be applied with mechanical rigidity. A judge, like a confessor, cannot hide behind his book and apply what he finds there with mechanical strictness; he must use his discretion.

There is a passage (although only in one manuscript) of the laws of Æthelred II which shows how far this

movement had gone. The influence of Archbishop Wulfstan is clear and the survival of some of his sermons shows
his strongly marked style. The date seems to be the very
beginning of the eleventh century (1008). This is what
he says:

And always, the greater a man's position in this present
life, or the higher the privilege of his rank, the more fully
shall he make amends for his sins, and the more dearly shall
he pay for all misdeeds; for the strong and the weak are not
alike, nor can they bear a like burden, any more than the
sick can be treated like the sound. And therefore in forming
a judgement, careful discrimination must be made between
age and youth, wealth and poverty, health and sickness and
the various ranks of life, both in the amends imposed by the
ecclesiastical authority, and in the penalties inflicted by the
secular law.

And if it happens that a man commits a misdeed involun-
tarily, or unintentionally, the case is different from that
of one who offends of his own free will, voluntarily and inten-
tionally; and likewise he who is an involuntary agent of his
misdeeds should always be entitled to clemency and better
terms owing to the fact that he acted as an involuntary agent.

Careful discrimination shall be made in judging every
deed, and the judgement shall always be ordered with justice,
according to the nature of the deed, and meted out in proportion, in affairs both religious and secular; and, through the
fear of God, mercy and leniency and some measure of for-
bearance shall be shown towards those who have need of
them. For all of us have need that our Lord grant us his
mercy, frequently and often. Amen.[1]

Those words are homiletic in tone, and their insertion
in the laws of Æthelred (and much matter to the same

---

[1] VI Æthelred 52; the translation is that of Miss A. J. Robertson,
Laws of the Kings of England (1925), p. 107.

effect in the laws of his successor, Cnut) can confidently be attributed to the influence of the famous Wulfstan[1] (who, like his successor Ælfric Puttoc, held simultaneously the two sees of York and of Worcester).

The Penitentials had done their work, sometimes by actual precept (for at times they impose in their tariffs heavier penances on persons of rank) and often by the inevitable spirit of comparison, doubt and distrust created by their very deficiencies, leading to the use of a wide discretion; as a result, in the last years of the Anglo-Saxon age, not only in the Church but also in the State, there was express recognition of the need to go further and deeper if there was to be a true tribunal of penance.

Some progress, moreover, had been made in the broader and still more fundamental field of the exploration of the concepts of crime and sin. It was no longer adequate to examine a Penitential or a law-book and apply its contents as they stood; anyone who tries to apply a system of law, whether it be in the internal or in the external forum, must be prepared to think, study, use his intelligence—in short, to exercise his discretion and his reason. The Church had first to learn, and then to teach, this crucial lesson. As far as England was concerned, all this was fully accomplished by the time of the Conquest. Wulfstan undoubtedly learnt the lesson, like many other higher clergy who were aware of the march of events, and he was so impressed by the new learning that he used his great position in the confidence of the Kings Æthelred and Cnut to secure the widest possible publicity for

[1] See F. M. Stenton, *Anglo-Saxon England*, pp. 451, 453-4.

the new doctrine—to do that, he secured the emphatic and moving pronouncement (which I have just quoted) to be inserted in the laws of the king. Already, by the close of the Anglo-Saxon period, a new and fresher spirit was in the air, a spirit of inquiry which had already discovered that 'looking it up in the book' is not the final answer, and that if you are so rash as to use more than one book, you will be faced with the duty of choosing between them and of using discretion.

There still lay, behind all this, the even more funda-mental question of How? Admitting that a man should use his reason and exercise his discretion, what is it that should guide him when faced by difficult questions? When something is done, at what point does it become something wrong? Wherein does the fault consist? What is it that distinguishes guilt from innocence? Is the answer the same in law as in morals? If not, why not? In short, what is it that makes some acts good and some bad? Clearly a man cannot use his discretion until he has at least thought about some of these things, and he cannot think about them for more than a moment or two before becoming aware that he is concerned with matters both difficult and extensive. There had been for centuries a body of learning upon this subject, and indeed there was a bewildering mass of contradictory doctrine upon this fundamental point. Things were not made easier by the fact that the Christian era had inherited, and cherished, an imposing body of ethical teaching from the Greeks of antiquity, and adding to this what could be learned from the Old Testament, and especially from the first Gospel in the New, there resulted a deep division of opinion which was typified by the conflict between St Bernard and Peter Abelard.

There was much to separate these men, so great and yet so different, but there is no need to consider here this heroic conflict, significant though it was for the future of religious and philosophical thought, save only for this one point, that of intention. As the debate developed and as more exact technical expressions came to be employed, so it became all the clearer that two diametrically opposite ideas of sin were now opposed to one another. To St Bernard,[1] standing in the patristic tradition, it seemed that an intention, however right, could not justify an action which was materially bad; to Abelard[2] (quoting Jeremiah at this point) the root of the matter was that God regards the innermost mind and punishes the sin, since he can see the intention and has no need to look at the act: on the other hand, it is 'human justice [that] is more concerned to punish acts rather than sins', is the tart comment of Abelard.[3] All this was no doubt encouraging for the advancement of philosophy and moral theology, but to the hard-pressed administrator, confessor or judge, clerical or lay, it was little help to be told to use his discretion when Penitentials were concerned, unless he were given a clear lead on so fundamental a matter, and not simply a controversy—however interesting in itself, or however eminent the contestants.

[1] Philippe Delhaye, *Le Problème de la conscience morale chez S. Bernard* (Namur, 1957), p. 80.

[2] Etienne Gilson, *L'Esprit de la philosophie médiévale* (Gifford Lectures), 2nd. ed. (Paris, 1944), pp. 329–30 (cf. Jeremiah xx. 12).

[3] Abelard, *Ethica: Scito te ipsum*, cap. VII, in Migne, *Patrologia Latina*, CLXXVIII, 648–9: Nos vero...ad opera maxime judicium nostrum vertimus, nec tam culpas.

That lead came soon, however, from the *Book of Sentences* of St Peter Lombard, bishop of Paris. In it, under the influence of Peter Abelard, the scholastic method was used, and this subjective rather than objective view of moral theology was adopted.[1] In the course of hardly more than a century English law had entered into the intellectual life of Europe and was greatly enriched, both giving and receiving. Her contribution to the penitential literature in the field of theology, and the public utterances of Wulfstan in the field of secular law, had raised difficulties in the use of discretion, but the appearance of Peter Lombard's *Sentences* did much to put theology upon a methodical basis, and before the century was over there was to be the University of Paris to work out the implications of the new dialectical method.[2]

At that very moment the twelfth century was bringing other problems, which were firmly turning our common law of crimes into a modern direction. In the first place, the Crown steadily grew in prominence and our criminal law (except in some of the boroughs) became centralised under the Crown, its judges, and the legal profession which was soon to come into existence. Further, the Crown, out of its strength and originality, was able to

[1] On the general course of this development, see chapter xvii 'Intention, Conscience et Obligation' in Gilson, *op. cit.* pp. 324 ff.

[2] Thus it passed from the *Sentences* to St Thomas Aquinas, whose conclusions on this point are very clearly explained by Victor Cathrein, *De bonitate et malitia actuum humanorum* (Louvain, 1926) commenting on the *Summa Theologica*, *quaestiones* 18 to 21 of the '*prima secundae*'; also on intent, cf. C. L. von Bar, *History of Continental Criminal Procedure* (Boston, 1916), pp. 152–3.

carry out far-reaching reform. *Bot* and *wer* and *wite* (at least in that form) had not survived the anarchy of Stephen and it was for Henry II to inaugurate vast new plans for newer procedures.

The centralisation of justice which he effected required the co-operation of experienced, competent and trustworthy officers. Over a long series of centuries it must have appeared to at least some of the kings and their officers that no reliance could be placed upon voluntary help unless it was closely supervised, and that it was useless to depend upon injured parties or their kin to maintain the difficult procedure of bringing a criminal to justice. The chances were at least even that such proceedings would be used as a means of oppression by the powerful instead of a means of prosecution and redress by the victims of crime. As for the expectation that injured parties would bring 'appeals' and engage in judicial combat with murderers, thieves, highwaymen and such like, all experience showed that there was nothing to be expected from that quarter. The only alternative was the employment of royal agents— sheriffs, coroners, escheators and bailiffs of many sorts (to say nothing of the numerous town officials, who had ample opportunities of manipulating criminal procedure behind the shelter of the town wall). If governments want to prosecute criminals they must do it themselves.

That is a question which lies at the root of medieval administration, civil as well as criminal, and the quality (as well as the quantity) of governmental activity must have largely depended upon its choice of agents, and the degree of its control over them. There are difficult problems in this connexion. As is well known, the Crown (through the exchequer and its vast and cumbersome machinery of writs and rolls) was able to keep a tight hold, of sorts, upon the sheriff, and would harass his descendants for generations after his death for real or supposed debts due to the Crown. It is not so clear that this resulted in any effective control over a sheriff at the time that he was engaged in some irregularity—for it is prompt action against a misdoer at as near a time to the misdeed as possible that will most effectively check irregularities. Proceedings against his children and grandchildren may be severe, and even productive of some revenue, but they will hardly serve to keep the sheriff upright in his dealings with the public. Indeed, the Crown's servants seem to have gained somewhat doubtful reputations, and it is well known that one of them, the escheator, is permanently commemorated in the English language (and in the language of criminal law) by the word 'cheat' which served to describe his activities. The Crown's county officials, therefore, were probably at best only an unreliable support in the heavy burden of government.

One of the most frequent duties of the sheriff and of his bailiffs was the impanelling of jurors both judicial and administrative. The immense increase of this sort of business dates from the close of the twelfth century, and is a reflection of the firm faith of the central departments in what the jury said, their constant use as a convenient means of getting that information which fills so many rolls still surviving today, and (especially in our subject) of the king's determination that presentment by a jury was sufficient to put a man on a trial of the gravest kind. This great revolution in our criminal procedure made other procedures, like the appeal and those procedures associated with 'hand-having and back-bearing thieves', look unmistakably ancient compared with the new indictment. The Assize of Clarendon[1] is a short, workmanlike document which contains crisp orders on how the thing is to work. Inquests were to be summoned in every county, hundred and vill; the sheriffs were to assemble the jurors, and they were to take charge of the accused persons whom the presenting juries revealed. The sheriff was to see that the peace machinery was in good order, and let no one, 'not even in the honour of Wallingford', try to exclude him from his land. The stern words of Henry II made it clear that the king through his sheriffs would assert the primacy of the Crown to control as a unified system the criminal law of the country.

Nevertheless, kings distrusted their sheriffs[2] and much else besides. Intellectual inquiry had cast a sense of doubt upon some venerable institutions, and Henry II publicly expressed his grave doubts about the ordeal.

By the middle of the century, when Henry II came to the throne, there was much that the author of the *Leges Henrici Primi* had tried to explain from his study of the Anglo-Saxon laws which was no longer relevant, and the drastic reforms of Henry II had swept away many relics of the Anglo-Saxon order. One that still remained

[1] (1166); text in Stubbs, *Charters* (9th ed.), pp. 170–3.
[2] Cf. the Inquest of Sheriffs, *ibid.* pp. 175–8; J. Tait, 'A new fragment of the Inquest of Sheriffs (1170)', *English Historical Review*, vol. xxxix, pp. 80–3; Lady Stenton, *Pleas before the King or his Justices* (Selden Soc., vol. 67), pp. 151–4.

was a survival from the past of very ancient date: the ordeals. The hot iron, which might be simple or triple, the cold water, the hot water, and the 'cursed morsel' (an ordeal reserved for clergy) were all ancient proceedings, but most of them frequently occur on the rolls even as late as the twelfth century; the religious accompaniments thought to be necessary have been collected from liturgical texts by Liebermann, and their appearances on the rolls have been described by Dr A. L. Poole in his *Obligations of Society*.[1]

These practices can only be described as irrational. They decide what later ages would call 'the general issue'—the broad question of 'guilty' or 'not guilty'. Decisions of that sort may be even now difficult to make: in days when the presentation of evidence and the appraisal of its effect were hardly known, it must have seemed a great comfort to throw the difficult burden upon providence and to trust the inanimate elements, duly consecrated, to reveal the truth. Doubts about the efficacy and even the theological legitimacy of the ordeals appeared in very high circles—Agobard, the saintly bishop of Lyons, had been outspoken about them as early as the days of Charlemagne (or shortly after).

Henry II in his own day (which we should remember as also the time when the treatise called 'Glanvill' was compiled) could in royal and public documents use language which must have shocked many people. Thus in the Assize of Clarendon of 1166 he lays down various

[1] With the works of Poole (1946) and Liebermann (1898–1916) cf. also H. C. Lea, *Superstition and Force* (3rd ed.), Philadelphia, 1878), and a large continental literature listed in R. C. van Caenegem, *Geschiedenis van het Strafprocesrecht in Vlaanderen* (Royal Flemish Academy, 1956).

rules for the presentment of suspects, their capture, their safe custody, and their subjection to the ordeal. Their lords may indeed 'replevy' them, but no one shall have his court of them but the king only. Finally they will be 'put to their law'—and that seems to mean the ordeal appropriate to their rank; Glanvill at this moment was about to explain that the free and the unfree go to different sorts of ordeal. Which ever sort it was, the king seems to have been unimpressed and was very reluctant to accept acquittal at the ordeal as at all conclusive. In c. 14 of the Assize he bluntly declares that those who are found 'clean' by their law, shall nevertheless (if they are believed to be thoroughly bad characters) forswear the lands of the king, and within eight days shall cross the seas and be treated as outlaws. The Assize concludes with the provision that it shall last during the king's pleasure—he must surely have been thinking of the Imperial dictum[1] that the Imperial pleasure has the force of law and that he intended this Assize to be in every sense of the word 'law'; and it is in that emphatic context that Henry II dared to banish for life, under pain of outlawry, and at eight days' notice, men who had proved their innocence by their success at the ordeal.

The nature of trial by ordeal, which Henry II so profoundly distrusted, is of great importance for the future history of the jury. Some fundamental matters derived from it are still with us today. Its essence, as we have already said, is that it was irrational. It spoke by

[1] *Dig.* 1. 4. 1; *Inst.* 1. 2. 6; cf. the modern formula '*La Royne le Veult*' which is still used to convert a parliamentary bill into statute law.

signs, but gave no reasons. The questions which one put to it had to be simple—in the sense that an answer of 'yes' or 'no' was sufficient to meet the situation. It made no attempt to take notice of the intention of the accused, or to enter into any of the subleties of criminal law as they are generally recognised in civilised systems today. There was no arguing with it, and it could not be persuaded to change its mind, nor to clarify its mind—it had not got a mind. This peculiar characteristic may be called its *inscrutability*; faced with a question, the ordeal will give an answer, but it is useless for us to ask by what process it had arrived at that conclusion. It would be hazardous to doubt the correctness of that answer—Henry II had asked questions and received, through his officers and the ordeals, divers answers as to which he reached some disquieting conclusions (which he published); most people would possibly have felt that there was something blasphemous about it. After all, the most solemn mode of referring to the ordeal in the liturgical books was by the title they habitually gave it: '*Judicium Dei*', the 'Judgement of God'. The kings and royal documents generally (including the lawyers) commonly referred to it as the 'law' which in certain circumstances the accused must 'make'. To say that a man under indictment for one of the gravest crimes shall be 'put to his law' does in fact associate the ordeal with Law itself and places it in the company of sacral and hardly intelligible things. Once again, it would be an impertinence to ask too many questions, and it would be inviting trouble to be at all free in criticising a time-honoured institution which both Church and State had openly approved.

71

The crisis came at the fourth Lateran Council of 1215, and there was fortunately upon the throne of St Peter the greatest of all the medieval popes, Innocent III. There were problems in plenty which beset the Church and all Christendom at that moment—the crusade, the Albigeois and so on—but there was time for a drastic decree which came at a very awkward moment, at least for England. By the eighteenth chapter of its decrees the clergy were forbidden to take part in judgements of blood, or to give the blessing for the ordeals of hot or cold water, or of hot iron. At least since the days of the Carolingians there had been doubts and questionings, and the 'practical men' such as Regino of Prüm at the opening of the tenth century, and Burchard of Worms a century later, were gravely concerned whether any feasible alternative could be found, so great was their fear of perjury.[1] A century later still, at the opening of the twelfth century, there were populous and forward-looking towns (especially in Flanders) which had expressly obtained the abolition of the ordeals within their walls. When Innocent III threw the weight of Rome, and its formal orders to the clergy, into the balance against them, the cause of the ordeals had already been on the decline for at least a century.

Neither the Pope nor the Council abolished the ordeals: but they could (and did) forbid the clergy to be present at them or to take any part in them. That was in the latter part of November 1215. It may be supposed that early in the new year of 1216 this and its other

[1] P. Fournier and G. Le Bras, *Collections canoniques*, vol. I, pp. 411–12.

decrees were well known in England; then in October 1216, King John died and was succeeded by the infant Henry III. The troubles of that time, with a French army actively campaigning in concert with the insurgent barons, and recognising Louis VIII as a king of England, had been sufficient to explain the preoccupation of King John with other matters; the accession of a boy of nine was a novelty in English history and left the country without a natural head to frame a policy to deal with the crisis treated by the decree of the Lateran Council. During the troubles of the civil war, the criminal machinery set up by Henry II (as far as it was possible for it to work) had been steadily accumulating in the prisons (such as they were) large numbers of suspects who had been denounced by the presenting juries set up by the Assize of Clarendon. There they were to await trial. But how? The victory of the Crown had made it incontestable that prosecutions upon indictment were Crown proceedings, and there was obviously no question of trial by battle against the king. There remained their 'law'—trial by whatever ordeal the court regarded as suitable to their social position, the nature of the charge and the degree of suspicion attaching to them. But the council of the Lateran had forbidden clergy to take part; and it was generally felt that such ordeals could not be validly conducted without their participation. Nothing, therefore, could be done. These men were not convicted; but they were certainly not acquitted; presenting juries had already 'defamed' them, in the technical sense of the word, and it could hardly be denied that they lay under a certain amount of suspicion. The famous writ of 1219 is very well known;[1] it proceeded on the principle that persons should be dealt with on the basis of the degree of suspicion against them. There were to be no hangings, for indeed there were no convictions. Only suspicion could be reasonably deduced from the indictors. It is patent that all this is temporary, and the writ promised the judges to send them fuller directions later on. It never did. The judges, faced with crowds of prisoners whom they could not try, were forced to improvise. After a certain amount of hesitation, and of picking (and perhaps choosing) among the crowd of presenting jurors who must have been present, there resulted the petty or trial jury. It needed diplomacy and perhaps a degree of high-handedness to get prisoners to put themselves upon a jury. The law would not force it upon them. When they did accept it, it must often have been a desperate appeal to the unknown. The old ordeal was deeply rooted in the traditions of the countryside; the use of the jury could hardly be different. The court asked a question; the answer came—from the iron or water, hot or cold. There was nothing rational about it; merely the physical reactions of a material object. No thought, no weighing of evidence, no forming of an opinion. But a result was obtained; someone was hanged, or perhaps acquitted (and we know from the Assize of Clarendon what Henry II thought[2] about those who were found 'clean by their law'). How that result was reached nobody knew, and nobody very much cared: was it not the

---

[1] *Patent Rolls, 1216–1225*, p. 186; C. E. Wells, in *Law Quarterly Review*, vol. xxx, pp. 97 ff.

[2] Above, p. 70.

judgement of God? One does not ask questions or pry curiously in such circumstances. The result is inscrutable. The ordeal is an appeal to the supernatural; was not the jury of exactly the same sort? It would not occur to the public (nor to most prisoners) that the jury was anything different from the ancient ordeal which it replaced. It gave a verdict, guilty or not guilty, and at least as far as the law was concerned, it was nobody's business how that verdict was reached. Like the ordeals, the jury also was inscrutable.

This transference to the trial jury in criminal cases of the characteristics of the ordeal was indeed natural and to be expected, seeing that its functions, suddenly thrust upon it at very short notice, were obviously those of the ordeal which it had to replace. Nevertheless, it was not entirely inevitable, and if there had been a firm lead from the government at the critical moment of King John's death it might easily have turned out that the decree of the Lateran could have helped us to a rational mode of trial to replace the vanished ordeal. On the civil side we had long been accustomed to the grand assize for the trial of right when the tenant so desired, and to the petty assizes (which were even compulsory) when recent questions of seisin and disseisin were in dispute— questions, moreover, which often had a strong criminal element. These proceedings seem to have always been of a rational nature, and unconnected with the ordeals. Since assizes and inquests were human they could err, and since they could err, there were means to review their verdicts—as there were also means of 'falsifying' the decisions or correcting the errors of judges. No doubt men hastily concluded that if mistakes had occurred they were the result of wickedness rather than of honest ignorance, and the penalties of attaint were very severe. The implication of all this was clear: assizes and inquests might give wrong verdicts and could be punished if they did.

Why did not the criminal jury follow the same course? Perhaps it would have done if there had been a vigorous king instead of a minor in the critical days following the Fourth Lateran Council. As it turned out we took the easiest course and treated the verdict of a jury as if it had been the outcome of an ordeal. Not until 1907 with the establishment of the Court of Criminal Appeal were the last vestiges which still attached to trials for felony finally removed from our law and the criminal jury finally lost that inscrutability which it inherited from the ordeals.

CHAPTER IV

EDWARD I AND CRIMINAL LAW

If we place ourselves at the opening of Edward I's reign, we shall be in a better position to judge the situation in which he found himself. There had been gains and losses, and it is by no means easy to discover whether the state of English criminal law was static or not, unless we can first determine the state of this 'profit and loss' account.

At least one gain was obvious and incontrovertible: the Crown had maintained its hold over those 'causes' or 'pleas' which Cnut had listed as his. The *Leges Henrici Primi* show their continuity—but subtly feudalised and expressed in the (to us) more familiar language of 'pleas of the Crown'. Our kings would not tolerate any feudatory 'having his court' of men accused and indicted of these major crimes.[1] From the early days of the twelfth century at latest, the fate of English criminal law was decided for the future: it was to be one, and uniform, and royal. Local variants were once no doubt numerous, and some of them may have survived, sheltered by the walls of the boroughs. The practice of sending royal commissioners on frequent tours to 'deliver the gaols' must have helped considerably to bring home to the local populace, be it in town or in country, that the law of crime was a 'common' law which cared little for local peculiarities: as Maitland was to remark, 'The common

[1] The expression occurs in the Assize of Clarendon, c. 15.

77

law was all for simplicity'—and necessarily the cult of simplicity brought with it the cult of uniformity.

This passion for simplicity will bring us to some matters which will seem to us disquieting, and will set us wondering whether we are not faced with 'loss' rather than 'profit'. That our law should be expressed in newer language—in French—need not surprise us. Our old Saxon law-words, like the names of our old Saxon saints, seemed outlandish, and certainly unpronounceable by Norman lips. Very probably, too, it was easier to achieve uniformity in a new language than in an old one which carried along with it so much history—indeed, local and provincial history. This language difficulty must have occurred all over the country; what concerns us at this moment, however, is not the philological question, but the more subtle semantic one. The 'pleas of the Crown' were not merely the old 'rights of the king', with French names instead of English ones. The newer expressions already had (or were soon to acquire) differences of meaning which were destined to change their character. The major crimes will for the future be classified under the word 'felony', and to that word there will be attached a number of adjuncts which will together constitute a body of uniform law. The penalty was meant to be uniform throughout the country. This may have been an ideal rather than a practice, but at least, the Crown did exercise a decisive influence upon it in spite of local peculiarities: thus there had long been concern at the indiscriminate use of the death penalty; in the laws of king Æthelred it is laid down that 'God's handiwork, which he redeemed at so great a price, ought not to be

EDWARD I AND CRIMINAL LAW

destroyed for trivial offences'. This feeling bore fruit in the next reign when William the Conqueror completely abolished the death penalty, substituting the even more savage, and generally fatal, penalty of mutilation.[1]

When the Crown was acknowledged as being particularly concerned with criminal law, as king, its directives upon the use of capital or other punishment were taken for granted as part of the exercise of its undoubted powers.

The restored use of the death penalty by Henry I[2] went far to simplify the law, but it carried simplicity to extremes, and it fixed upon our criminal law a classification which for centuries made it impossible to reach a satisfactory analysis of offences or of penalties. It has often been asked why our law was so prodigal of the death sentence. The speculation of Maitland was that our old legal system called for the payments of so many and such large sums of money that the whole system broke down because there were few who could raise them. This system spelt disaster to many people, especially the criminal, for it seems assumed that if he cannot or will not pay, then his life is forfeit. Others suffered also: lords who had legitimate expectations of substantial windfalls were disappointed. So were others, too. The kinsmen of a slain man now stood little chance of receiving a *wer* in the face of so much competition from different quarters. It is indeed true that as early as the end of the seventh century it had been

---

[1] *Hic Intimatur*, c. 10: Stubbs, *Charters* (9th ed.), p. 99; Liebermann, *Gesetze*, vol. I, pp. 486.

[2] Florence of Worcester, *Chronicle*, vol. II, p. 57: Stubbs, *Charters*, p. 113.

necessary in one case, at least, to give priority to the *wer* over the *wite*,[1] but we seem never to have got any further than that. The almost inevitable insolvency of criminals faced with all these demands completely defeated our law. Their fate varied from time to time. In times and at places where the death penalty was in force, there was an easy way out; failing that, there must have been many who were reduced to slavery or serfdom—especially when under the early Norman kings the death penalty had been removed. Still others took to the woods, and lived the life of outlaws.

A loss to theory, as well as to the sufferers from crime, was the pre-emptive practice of the Crown in the matter of forfeitures. The new feudal criminal law was succinctly explained in the *Dialogus de Scaccario* II, 16 thus: One who has offended against the king may (*a*) lose all his chattels for a minor offence; or (*b*) lose all his lands and rents, and be disinherited, for greater matters; or (*c*) for great 'enormities' he will lose life or members. Maitland may be right in saying that this is 'too simple', in some cases at least; but there can be no doubt that events were moving in that direction.[2] In the competition for such money as was to be had, the Crown was a favoured competitor, even when it was ranged (as it sometimes was) against ecclesiastical or civic authorities.

There was one chance where the old law survived, and that was the appeal of larceny. This ancient proceeding served a double purpose. If the plaintiff was successful,

---

[1] Ine 71.
[2] Pollock and Maitland, vol. II, p. 459, n. 1.

he convicted the thief and also got back the stolen goods; it was (incidentally to the crime) a real action for the recovery of the chattels. In this form, the appeal was almost disconcertingly reasonable: the convicted thief was hanged, and having discharged this duty, the plaintiff went home with the goods. Surely he had deserved the goods, for he had fought and executed the culprit. The Crown did not venture to attack this institution directly; but it provided a substitute—the indictment. The Crown soon furnished it with a theory (which of course worked to the benefit of the king). It was essentially a royal proceeding, in which the injured party took little part. He was not called upon to fight; neither did he get back the stolen goods. There is no doubt what happened to them—they went to the king. The convicted thief forfeited all he had, which included (as Maitland pointed out) all that he seemed to have as well.[1] Since he forfeited the stolen goods, the law was led in the course of time to the curious conclusion that a thief had acquired property in them by his crime. It could, of course, be plausibly maintained that it was the victim's remissness which compelled the Crown to bring its own indictment proceedings in default of an appeal of larceny, and that therefore the loser need not expect to find sympathy from the Crown. This curious argumentation lasted until the statute of restitution[2] of Henry VIII in 1529. The situation during the Middle Ages was that the victim

---

[1] And hence goods which were in his hands only as bailee; see the comments on the forfeiture of his master's goods by a servant who has incurred forfeiture in Plucknett, *Concise History of the Common Law* (5th ed.), p. 474; statute of staples, 27 Ed. III, st. 2, c. 19.

[2] 21 Henry VIII, c. 11.

of a theft had little to hope unless (by his own endeavours) he discovered the thief, appealed him, defeated him in battle, and thereupon hanged him. Failing that, the stolen goods went to the king, if the thief was prosecuted on indictment.

What had been abundantly clear to the Anglo-Saxons—that the victim of a theft ought to get his property back—seemed of only secondary importance as the age became more thoroughly feudal and royal. If the owner did not relish fighting for his property and disposing of the thief, then he could abandon it, and leave it to the king. The king would proceed by indictment, hang the thief (that is what kings are for), and draw his modest fee—the culprit's pots and pans, and, of course, the stolen goods.

There might be other wrongdoing which did not involve theft: for example, there was the very wide and important field of personal injuries. Here the Anglo-Saxon law had its own simple and (within limits) sensible solution. To the injured man it gave balm for his wounds—at so much an inch; to the Church and local magnates it gave payments (quite substantial payments) in respect of disorder and fighting in their houses, and other affronts to holy places and distinguished men. Was all that to go, too, together with the queerly-named payments which the laws set out? Not entirely, and not everywhere. A passage among the customs of Preston in the twelfth century shows clearly what might happen in a town where the old ideas and procedures were still cherished. If one burgess wounds another, we are told, and they are ready to accept the mediation of their friends, the settlement shall be at the rate of 4*d.* an inch, *plus* the medical costs, and also the consequential damage due to the wound, and an oath that if the position were reversed, the one who pays would have received that money (with the advice of his kin) as a reasonable settlement.[1] The old pre-Conquest ideas seem to be just on the point of turning into damages. It is true that the Preston custumal is thinking more of 'good offices' than of litigation; nevertheless it is clear that an action for trespass which ended in a judgement for damages could hardly have seemed strange or unnatural to burgesses accustomed to that procedure. It may well be believed that the Anglo-Saxon *bot* in a new guise was to produce one of the most characteristic elements in the new action of trespass.

When Edward I came to the throne after the troubles of the civil war, one naturally thinks of Henry II bringing his reign of stern law and order after the anarchy of Stephen. Edward I, like his great-grandfather, was to find in legislation both his fame in history and his practical contribution to the law and institutions of his contemporaries. He was not the first to legislate, and the traditional collection of statutes which every lawyer trusted generally began with the Great Charter of 1225.[2] That already venerable document contained words which indicate the criminal problem, not only of the young Henry III, but also of Edward I. In c. 17 it gets very near to the root of the matter when it enacts that

[1] *Borough Customs* (Selden Society, vol. 18), I, pp. 30–1.
[2] That is to say, the fourth (the others being those of 1215, 1216 and 1217).

6-2

'no sheriff, constable, coroners or other bailiffs of ours may hold pleas of our crown'. There was still, no doubt, the perpetual need for 'the man on the spot' to keep criminal law moving; and there was the equally perpetual danger that the man on the spot will be tempted to 'hold' pleas of the Crown for his own benefit instead of merely 'keeping' them for trial by judges or other officials authorised by the central government. It was only by the constant interplay of justices of the peace acting under statute, royal commission, the control of the central courts, and faced and checked by the competition of other bodies of commissioners, that it finally became possible to solve one of the most persistent and difficult of the problems of government, namely the reconciliation of central and local institutions; that problem was constantly present in the mind of Edward I and of his successors.

Edward I's legislative policy has a few antecedents in the laws of his predecessors, but for the most part it is an independent construction of the king himself and his advisers, and it is in those statutes that we must find his ideas and policy.

Edward I enjoyed the luxury of not having to hurry home and fight, or intrigue, for his inheritance; he stayed abroad on the crusade, and did not return to England until August 1274. At his first Parliament he caused to be enacted the First Statute of Westminster (1275) containing some fifty-one chapters, many of them (though not quite all) being concerned with the criminal law. These chapters succeed one another in no discernible order, but when they are arranged in a rough

classification, it becomes clear what were the problems
to which Edward directed his first statute.

There were several chapters dealing with purveyance,
which was a delicate subject: it was a royal prerogative,
and vitally important in an emergency; yet it was easily
abused, and became a potent instrument of oppression
in the hands of officials and castellans. It raised the
general problem of the Crown's relations with its subor-
dinate officers and their bailiffs—and this was a point
to which Edward I often returned in the course of this
statute. The mild reminder that the Justices at Westminster ought to finish the day's work before com-
mencing anything new (c. 46) takes a more sinister
aspect when it is read with other chapters in the same
statute which deal with the clerks of justices and others
who extort by means of making charges for copies of the
chapters to be delivered to jurors, or by getting themselves presented to a litigious church or otherwise
committing fraudulent practices in connexion with litigation in the courts. The clerks of the justices were not
alone in these misdeeds. The serjeants at law, the leaders
of the bar, were threatened with imprisonment and
disbarment if they beguiled the court or a party.

The counterparts of the sheriffs were the coroners,
and this statute laments that the office often falls to mean
and indiscreet men. The casual mention in it of some of
the things a coroner was supposed to do, shows how
much the Crown entrusted to these officials, and what a
disaster it would be if the Crown did not succeed in
getting suitable candidates for the post, or in maintaining
strict control over them when they were appointed. It

was, of course, the sheriff who came in for most attention in the statute. Thus c. 9 has almost an Anglo-Saxon ring in it when it commands all people to be in readiness and appareled, to pursue felons, for experience had shown the need of fresh suit and the possibility of obstruction being caused by franchises—to say nothing of sheriffs who from fear, or favour, or by corruption, or for affinity, do not act vigorously and honestly when their friends ought to be arrested and kept until their trial. Sheriffs were suspected of other misdeeds also, such as partial (or 'favourable') inquests when men suspected of homicide brought writs *de Odio et Atia*; of failing to discharge those who had paid them moneys due to the king, so that the exchequer continued to pursue them for payment; and of allowing their county courts to be manipulated by 'barrators and maintainers of quarrels' (and in this connexion it is notable that 'the stewards of great lords' are expressly brought under suspicion). Indeed, coroners, sheriffs and judges do not exhaust the list: in c. 2 the king admonishes the prelates (thus he expressed himself) that a clerk convicted of felony and delivered to the ordinary, shall in no wise be allowed to depart until he has performed his canonical purgation, as his defence in a church court was called.

Most of this, as will be seen, raises in one form or another the crucial question of the dependability of the Crown's officers and the grave danger that the Crown would bear the odium for the misdeeds of its underlings. Nearly a quarter of a century later, in 1298, these problems were still causing acute anxiety in government circles, and the edition of an assize roll of that year by the late Dr Thomson for the Lincoln Record Society strikingly illustrates the endeavour of Edward I to check the excesses of his purveyors, local bailiffs, sheriffs and administrators. There can be little doubt that, in his eyes, the problem of criminal law was very largely the problem of getting vigorous and honest men in the lower ranks of the official hierarchy, for it was they who most often came into close touch with the people, and had most opportunities of becoming petty tyrants.

Nevertheless, there were other factors, and the first Statute of Westminster was well aware of them. Apart from the question of enforcement, there was the content of the law itself. Was it adequate? Was it of a sort to strike a sensible onlooker as being fair?

We may agree (with some sympathy for the king in his heavy task) that a parliamentary statute cannot always be expected to deal finally with a situation which in fact was a permanent (though disreputable) feature of medieval life, but it could do a great deal to mould, to correct, and to strengthen the body of legal doctrine which dealt with crime. It was exactly that sort of reform which seems to have been most apt for parliamentary legislation. It is true that Parliament was not entirely a novice in this art, and it is abundantly proved that the parliaments of Edward I could work hard and courageously in the field of property and mercantile law. The great line of statutes from *De Donis* to *Quia Emptores* clearly showed what could be done by a vigorous and very skilful government which intended to reduce our private law to a workable order. Why did they not do as much for criminal law?

This is a puzzling feature of medieval legal history, upon which there is less light than one could wish. Certainly the contrast when compared with the development of property law and the resourcefulness of its exponents is abundantly shown by the nature of the legislation upon it (especially in the reign of Edward I) and by the ingenuity of the debates upon it reported in the Year Books. Nor need we over-blame Bracton. There was now on the bench a generation which could have been (and probably was) trained in the technique of law in Bracton's treatise. Most of that work is devoted, it is true, to the elaboration of real property, and he did not live to complete his plan and deal with contract and tort. He did deal, however, in some measure with criminal law. It was necessarily centred upon the king and his pleas and its treatment is largely procedural; much of it, indeed, is devoted to the duties of the various officers—sheriffs, coroners and the like—whose office brought them into contact with criminal law and the travelling justices of various sorts who administered it on behalf of the king.

Statutes do not necessarily proceed always from the same source as the more considered works of legal learning, and Parliament did not represent the more technical aspects of the law except upon special occasions when those who were learned in the law were at hand to prompt it. For the most part it seems to have been influenced principally by laymen, who no doubt were experienced in these matters, but evidently could not be regarded as legal experts. It is largely to them, rather than to the lawyers, that we must attribute this legislation. That they were active is beyond all doubt. There is, for example, the Statute of Winchester of 1285 which is principally concerned with the urban rather than the rural aspects of crime, and comes significantly enough from the Parliament which was also the author of the Statute of Merchants (although it may be that there were no Commons summoned). The first chapter explains that the king regards the fear of a statutory penalty as more effective than the sanction of an oath—a significant admission, surely—and repeats his command that fresh suit must be made against felons. The second chapter contains a principle strongly reminiscent of Anglo-Saxon law, for it enacts that the hundred where the robbery was committed shall be answerable for the loss and for the damages, unless they can produce the offender. This liability of the hundred for robberies done within its borders strongly suggests the similar rule making it responsible for the murders of Normans—again, unless they can produce the culprit. This tendency to hold the hundred responsible for undetected crimes became a favourite device with parliaments. Nor was it original to Edward I, for when Henry III had proposed to enact such a rule in 1253, it was denounced as an innovation from Savoy.[1]

This imposition of a vicarious liability upon a unit of local government which had failed in its duty under the criminal law, was certainly a strong measure; there were others in the same statute which repeated or reinforced earlier laws which imposed duties of watch and ward in cities and boroughs, the keeping of suitable

[1] See the references in Pollock and Maitland, vol. I, p. 181.

weapons and armour to be used by those who are thus required to keep the peace, and especially the remarkable provision of its fifth chapter that the highway from one merchant town to another shall be cleared so that no cover for malefactors should be allowed for a width of two hundred feet on either side; landlords who do not effect this clearance will be answerable for robberies committed in consequence of their default, and in case of murder they will be in the king's mercy.

All these provisions are more directed to the general problem of enforcement than to the actual content of the criminal law. The passages in which they more nearly concern themselves with the substance of the law are few and are comparatively unimportant. We do not find under Edward I precise and technical definitions of crimes; the most his statutes contain is procedural details, and very occasionally, the specification of penalties.

A most striking feature of our older criminal law and legislation is its reluctance to use imprisonment; even when it does appear, it is often merely a means to the end of extracting money from the offender. A fixed term, imposed as a penalty, seems to be a novelty—and a rare one—in Edward I's legislation, where it seems reserved for those cases which aroused indignation; thus poaching incurs three years *plus* a fine, and ultimately outlawry;[1] a bailiff of a franchise who does not pursue a felon may get one or two years,[2] and the lawyer, be he the eminent serjeant-at-law or any other, who is guilty of any manner of deceit in the king's court may get a 'year at least'.[3]

---

[1] Westminster I, c. 20.   [2] *Ibid.* c. 9.
[3] *Ibid.* c. 29.

Occasionally the statute has had a curious history. Thus the 'hard and strong prison' (*prisone forte et dure*) of Westminster I, chapter 12 became the '*peine forte et· dure*' by which those who refused to plead were crushed to death, but died unconvicted (although in terms the statute only applied to notorious felons and did not apply to those 'taken on light suspicion ').

There is a good deal of matter which could logically be mentioned here, although it would not contain much that bears upon what has already been said. It would seem that beneath the large mass of detail which is already available in the statutes, the Year Books, and (although much less) in printed plea rolls, the most significant factor was rather the change of atmosphere and training in the legal profession. From Bracton we get abundant detail, careful arrangement, and a scientific approach which shows clearly in everything he wrote, although it is occasionally obscured by the mischances which befell his text. This stately Latin treatise was followed by works of a different kind. The Latin of the canonist and civilian was replaced by the French of the steward and bailiff (to say nothing of the serjeant-at-law and the lesser ranks of the profession) and by smaller, but still very interesting little tracts upon a variety of subjects. There is one which is entirely on criminal law, *Le Ple de la Corone*, but it has never yet been printed; some of the tracts edited by Maitland for the Selden Society many years ago under the title of *The Court Baron* deal with matter which is largely, but not entirely, criminal. It is natural that literature of that class should devote itself to criminal matters because it was evidently used and appreciated by people who were much engaged in keeping courts and doing the necessary, but unpleasant, work of prosecuting offenders in the manorial court of their lord. They were most at home in French rather than Latin literature. The language question soon settled down; our law became French. The literature of the law (notably the Year Books) also became French, and we abandoned the more academic and international Latin of the thirteenth century.

This cut us off from the mainstream of continental learning which was generally in Latin (unless it was addressed to a purely local public of some particular fief, such as many of the French custumals). On the other hand, it threw open some elementary but practical little books which, being in French, were not confined to the learned class. In particular, it put the literature of the later common law (and there was very little of it anyhow) within the reach of the growing class which was literate, to the extent of reading French and being interested in the practical side of criminal law especially as it affected the tenants of a manor whether it be within the manor, or before the king's judges when they delivered the gaols, held assizes, courts of *oyer* and *terminer* or the like. It was a useful and influential class, extending from the lowly reeve or bailiff right up to the governing class which spoke French; the class in fact which sent knights of the shire, citizens and burgesses to sit in Parliament.

It is the remarkable unanimity which we find among judges, serjeants, civil servants (of the more modern departments), members of the king's council, the ruling classes, members of Parliament—people in authority generally—which is so remarkable and so significant. It was indeed a bond of union between them; but it was also a wall of separation which kept them equally apart from the academic, clerical and Latin side of English life. Above all, it cut us off from the universal world of learning and thought which expressed itself, not in a national language, but in Latin where the civilian and canonist, theologian and lawyer and political theorist could speak freely to his like all over the Christian world.

This is not the place to consider the course of English legal education and the rise of those remarkable institutions, the Inns of Court; yet we are bound to mention them, because their outlook is so radically different from that of the universities, and their tradition rapidly became nationalistic, anti-academic, and fiercely opposed to the civilians and canonists. These prejudices are displayed in some detail by a Chief Justice of England, Sir John Fortescue, who wrote his 'Praises of the Laws of England' in or near the year 1470. The attitude in question was fully developed by the time that Fortescue wrote, and he entirely shared the views and prejudices of his contemporaries; he has abundant praise for the Inns of Court, and magnifies the office which he held (save for an interval during his troubles in the Wars of the Roses). He also loudly vaunts the laws of England at the expense of those of other lands—especially France—who do not enjoy the blessing of living under them. We can hardly accuse Fortescue of total ignorance, but it does seem fair to attribute Fortescue's quotations to the use of anthologies and dictionaries of quotations rather than to his acquaintance with the works in their original form.

His overriding interest seems to have been political science and his devotion to that monarchy which he distinguishes as 'political' instead of absolute. His blending of nationalism, enthusiasm for the jury, loyalty to the Inns of Court, distrust of foreigners, the universities, and his willingness to get help (when he deemed it useful) from theological arguments, seems to show that the typical English attitude towards civilian and canonist was already reduced to a system in the days of Fortescue. The separation of English law which was already appearing from the days of Wyclif had now become deeper, and for the future was to become the general traditional attitude of English lawyers. It is true that this attitude is conspicuous, and displayed in its most finished form, in the life and works of Fortescue; nevertheless it was long being prepared, and it is suggested that it first appeared in England when we abandoned the Bractonian tradition, expressed our law in French, ceased to frequent the universities and resigned ourselves to a process of self-education which is now being traced for us by Professor S. E. Thorne in his illuminating researches into the Readings and Moots of the Inns of Court. Its origin should therefore be placed at least as early as the appearance of those *Four Law Tracts* which the late Professor Woodbine attributed to the last years of old Bracton—say, about the year 1260.

In matters of thought, belief, learning, art, science—matters of the spiritual side of man in the broader sense of the word—intellectual divisions may well be disastrous. Divisions were nevertheless welcomed in England, and the Crown took the early opportunity of uniting its own interests with those of its nobles and gentry by weaving one body of property law, entrusted to the keeping of one judicial system (at least until the fifteenth century when the emergence of chancery and star chamber brought us troubles), and expounded by one legal profession educated, not at the universities, but at the Inns of Court. Such a situation is bound to foster conservatism which may be profound and deep-rooted, although it is less likely to be adventurous or militant. In the nature of things, it made for divisions, and we must count our losses. We ceased even to read civil and canon literature. The professions which needed those studies as the tools of their trade drifted away and in the fourteenth century the common law was truly isolated.

Stimulated by the growth of the universities, both civilian and canonistic studies attracted able and original men whose voluminous productions were little known to common lawyers, and yet the things which civilians and canonists studied might well have contributed to our criminal law. Thus there were numerous studies of procedure which showed how thought was turning into the useful direction of considering the functions and objects of procedure, and of criticising existing institutions from the point of view of their adequacy in the light of those researches.

Canonists also had devoted considerable thought to some of the problems of criminal law, notably to the aim and object of penalties. They thus distinguished some penalties as vindictive, their main object being to repress the crime; others seem rather to be in the nature of intimidation, designed primarily to dissuade people from certain conduct; yet others seemed directed principally to the reformation of the offender. In practice, a single penalty might partake in varying degrees of all these objects. Starting from this analysis it was possible to frame ample theories of the nature and purpose of penalties, and some very remarkable results followed. To most of the older bodies of law it seemed unsuitable to impose imprisonment for any purpose except that of securing the presence of a person when wanted; it should not be used as a punishment. Clearly enough, the expenditure of board and lodging in order to keep a prisoner in idleness seemed to the Romans quite illogical. It required a certain degree of courage to maintain a different view in the face of the high authority accorded to Ulpian.[1] Nevertheless, by a different line of reasoning, and pursuing a different penal theory, the Church began to admit imprisonment as a punishment, as well as a means of preventive detention. It developed from the idea of penance, and as we learn from the Penitentials they could have as their object something distinctly spiritual, namely the confinement of a man so as to be alone with his conscience, without the distractions of ordinary life. In such a condition he could at leisure come to a proper estimate of his fault, and attain that state of mind which the Church required.

Such an imprisonment was possible for the Church much more than for the lay power, since the Church had monasteries where persons could be confined, and fed (but not very much), and kept under ecclesiastical supervision. It was inevitable that in time the Church

[1] *Dig.* 48. 19. 8, 9.

should find it necessary to maintain prisons, especially for those convicted of heresy. The Church soon pronounced a sentence of a determinate duration—here again the similarity with the ancient Penitentials with their fixed terms of penances is remarkable.

The canonists were not the only ones who produced speculations about crime which we ought to have studied, and did not. There were the civilians, and one of the numerous army of writers on the imperial laws was Lucas de Penna. His doctrine and writings are carefully examined in Dr Walter Ullmann's important work *The Medieval View of Law* (London, 1946). Civilian as he was, he nevertheless enjoyed the freedom which common lawyers had lost, of consulting the works of many authors in different faculties, and his legal doctrine is much enriched by his close knowledge of St Thomas Aquinas. Thus, as an example, he takes the view that Abelard had maintained, on the place of intention as the prime element in crime.

Lucas, moreover, deals with a matter which was of capital importance: the problem of proof. Our old Anglo-Saxon laws and certain practices in the Middle Ages had been sacral in origin, and to the end of the story and later, had imposed upon us a system of proof which (at least in its early days) had revealed its nature and origin because it was 'inscrutable' as I have ventured to call it. This problem of proof is one which has fascinated legal historians for nearly a century, and lawyers for many centuries. On the continent the approach was strictly scientific—and that involves measurement and figures. The principle was that a complete proof could be represented by the figure 'one' or unity. But in real life we rarely get more than partially convincing evidence—in other words, only fractions of unity. Nevertheless, it is quite possible to add the fractions together, and when they add up to unity it simply means that there were a number of facts, each of them alone being of merely fractional weight, although taken all together, those fractions will prove a point—and mathematically speaking, that means that they will add up to unity. This system lasted in some places and in some jurisdictions until the nineteenth century.

It has been abandoned. But much thought went to its elaboration. Every piece of evidence had to be weighed and given its fractional value. The whole operation implied an earnest attempt to work out a calculus of proof, to be scientific, to be fair, to get at the truth. It may have been mistaken, but we must allow that the men who elaborated it were not idle, nor heedless of the problems which they as legal practitioners had to face and solve as best they could.

All that has carried us far from Edward I. It would be unjust to blame him, for he could hardly have known the ultimate effects of his policy. We have to use our great advantage in time in order to display what seems to be the significance of the events of his reign. That movement for French instead of Latin as the language for law-books was ominous. A nation may well be peculiar and develop its law along the lines which history has suggested to it; but need it be—ought it to be—isolated?

There was more than that. We cannot speak seriously

about Edward I without saying something about Parliament. A momentous result of his policy was to throw criminal law into the hands of Parliament. This was another facet of the change of language which is the external sign of what was happening in these events. The members of Parliament with their preference for French were obviously the important men back in their counties, and their careers were passed in administration (and sometimes war)—in either case among the men who were increasingly lay, and increasingly apathetic to the Bractonian, learned, academic tradition. The cosmopolitan learning of civilian and canonist passed them by: for men of this sort the future lay with the Year Books and certain little French tracts (which indeed were good in their way).[1]

When we say this, it seems clear what was in Maitland's mind when he associated the fall of Bractonism with the rise of Parliament.[2] He must have been thinking (although he did not elaborate the point) of the new spirit in the growing legal profession, so closely connected with the French-speaking governing class in both town and country, and with French-speaking stewards and bailiffs in the manors and French-speaking serjeants-at-law in Westminster Hall. Looking forward to the 'oracle of the law' he could see the meaning which gave some sort of sense to certain apparently stupid remarks which have gone down in history; thus Sir Edward Coke opines (in his preface to his *First Institute*) that Littleton's *Tenures*

---

[1] On all this, cf. Plucknett, *Early English Legal Literature* (1958), chap. v.
[2] Maitland, *Bracton's Note Book*, vol. i, pp. 6–7; Plucknett, *Concise History of the Common Law* (5th ed. 1956), pp. 264–5.

were 'the most perfect and absolute work that ever was written in any human science'; this same Coke tells James I that it does not matter that God should have so richly endowed His Majesty with reason, for our common law is an artificial reason; Coke further assures his readers that in England men are tried by jury, not by witnesses—by the old inscrutable ordeal-substitute which one accepted in faith, asking no questions.

The meaning was clear, and had been in course of preparation for some centuries—we were cut off from the rest of the world, and it was only in the peculiar atmosphere of the common law that Coke's sayings were intelligible.

Finally, the close understanding between these men and the common lawyers had the effect of throwing criminal law into a legislature. That legislature could at least register the great statutes of Edward I, especially those on the technicalities of real property law. Behind those statutes were men with a firm grasp of a tightly-knit system of strongly feudalised land law. The statute of merchants was a success—eventually.[1] The statute of Winchester made a brave show of dealing with the social and police problems of crime; but to criminal law Edward I's parliaments contributed nothing. The one solid point in criminal law was the indictment procedure of Henry II and the subsidiary machinery which went with it. In time, no doubt, we would gain a certain benefit when parliamentary legislation came before the

---

[1] The statute of Acton Burnell of 1283 had to be replaced by that of 1285, and the system needed some revision in the statute of staples: see T. F. T. Plucknett, *Legislation of Edward I*, pp. 138 ff.

courts, to be construed and interpreted like other legislation. It was that process that in the end was to give us
statutory definitions of crimes; that at least was a tremendous boon, for it had taught Parliament to frame its
legislation with the greatest of care and precision.

That sort of situation, however, prevented the courts'
building up a doctrine of criminal law as they had done of
property law. If the common lawyers had been stimulated by continental speculations into building up a body
of criminal law, just as they had been goaded by the
Crown and the landowners into putting our property
law into order, we might have had great consolidating
statutes in the Middle Ages instead of having to wait
until a hundred years ago. But that was not to be. When
criminal matters came before Parliament there seems to
have been no firm body of doctrine with an organised
profession to impose it merely by its prestige; instead, it
fell into the hands of amateurs. The justices of the peace
had at least practical experience, but their handiwork
was a vast disorderly mass of enactments of constantly
growing complexity, the despair of anyone who tried to
make sense out of it. In the end there came inevitably
the reform of our criminal law, but it needed the great
reform movement of the nineteenth century. In the
meantime, we had been paying a heavy price for our
isolation from all that the rest of Christendom could
have given us, and for having sent our criminal law to
Edward I's new parliament instead of to courts which
would have been encouraged to breathe the fresh air
of European learning.

INDEX

Abelard, Peter, 64–5
Acton Burnell, statute of, 100
Ælfric Puttoc, 62
Æthelberht, King, 7–12, 30–1
Æthelred, King, 60–2, 78
Æthelstan, King, 33, 55, 60
Agobard, Bishop, 69
Aldhelm, Abbot, 4
Alfred, King, 10, 12–16, 32–3, 53
amercement, 47, 52
Anglo-Saxon age, 28
Anglo-Saxon laws, ch. i, 37, 45–6, 51, 53, 92, 97
appeals of felony, 66, 80–1
Aquinas, Thomas, 97
attaint, 76

Bailment, 81
battle, trial by, 66
Bernard, St, 64–5
bot, 11, 17, 22, 51, 66
  and damages, 82–3
Bracton, Henry de, 5–6, 88, 91, 99
Breviarium Alaricianum, 4
Burchard of Worms, 72

Canonists, 95
Church
  on repentance, 23
  and imprisonment, 96
  Merovingian, 52, 57
  insular, or Roman, 54
  see also ordeals
Clarendon, Assize of, 69–70
Cnut, King, 10, 27, 29, 37, 39, 44, 77
Coke, Sir Edward, 99–100
Common Informers Act (1951), 32
Commutation of penance, 57
Coroners, 85
Court Baron, 91
criminal or civil, 24

Crown in criminal law, 24, 27, 29–34, 52, 65–7, 77–9
  described in *Leges Henrici Primi*, 46–50
  its officers, 85–7

Damages, 83
death penalty, 78–9
Decretum (of Ivo), 39
devils, 39
dialectic, 65
discretion, 57–8, 60–2, 64

Edmund, King, 20
Edward the Confessor, 27, 29, 37, 39, 44
Edward I, 1–3, 43, 77, 87–9, 98, 100
escheator, 67
extortion, 85

Feud, 19–21, 55
feudalism, 38, 41–6, 80
fine, see *wite*
forfeiture, 47, 52, 80
Fortescue, Sir John, 93–4
franchises, 27–9, 37–8, 41–3, 47, 90
French, 52, 78, 91–2, 98–9

Gilds, 19, 21
Glanvill, 5–6, 24

Henry I, 46–7, 79
Henry II, 27–8, 49, 66, 68–71, 73, 100
Henry III, 73, 89
hundred, 89

Imprisonment, 90, 96
indictment, 49, 100
Ine, King, 12, 32
informers, 31–2

103

For EU product safety concerns, contact us at Calle de José Abascal, 56–1°, 28003 Madrid, Spain or eugpsr@cambridge.org.

www.ingramcontent.com/pod-product-compliance
Ingram Content Group UK Ltd.
Pitfield, Milton Keynes, MK11 3LW, UK
UKHW012333130625
459647UK00009B/261